How to
GET
THINGS
DONE

hamlyn

How to
GET
THINGS
DONE

Organize your life
and achieve the
results you want

Ann Jackman

A Pyramid Paperback

First published in Great Britain in 2006 by Hamlyn,
a division of Octopus Publishing Group Ltd
2–4 Heron Quays, London E14 4JP

This material was previously published as *How to Get Things Done*

ISBN 0 600 61321 6
EAN 9780600613213

A CIP catalogue record for this book is available
from the British Library

Printed and bound in China

10 9 8 7 6 5 4 3 2 1

CONTENTS

Introduction 6

SECTION 1 **KNOWING YOURSELF** 12

SECTION 2 **KEY SKILLS FOR ACHIEVING SUCCESS** 34

SECTION 3 **10 STAGES TO SUCCESS** 92

SECTION 4 **PRACTICAL EXERCISES** 118

Index 142

Acknowledgements 144

Introduction

What motivates us to start up projects and make changes in our lives and work? Have you ever wanted to make changes or start projects but have failed to get them off the ground? Perhaps you have had a good idea and started planning how you are going to achieve it, but quickly lost interest after you considered more carefully how much work would be involved. Alternatively, you may feel that you have got neither the skills nor the imagination to make the changes that you want to make.

Increasingly, most of us have less time to do the things we really want to do. We are driven by the fast pace of the world around us, and the demands of others, both at work and in other areas of our lives. Yet we seem to want to achieve more. We are surrounded by images of people who have successful lives and beautiful homes. We are told that it is easier than ever to have it all. But how do we achieve this?

Many of us want to make changes in our lives and work. Some of us may want to make a career move, as we feel we have become stale in our current job. Others may want to build an extension to their home, to create additional space. Whatever the project we have in view, we need to be able to plan it and see it through to the end.

Case studies – Nigel and Pat

Here are two examples of changes that the people involved wanted to initiate.

For 10 years Nigel has planned his retirement in a rural area. He will achieve it next year following a series of well-planned steps. Not everything has gone smoothly; for example, poor performance in the stock market made it necessary for him to make last-minute changes to his retirement plan, and to adjust his goals for purchasing a property in the area in which he wanted to live. However, because of his determination to see his plan through to the end, Nigel has faced and overcome the barriers that threatened to sabotage his project.

Pat worked for 15 years in a large public-sector organization, where she was promoted to a senior management position. Following her last promotion, she received training as an internal organizational development (OD) consultant, a role that she enjoyed and developed for 3 years. However, because of the organization's career-development policy, her next posting within the organization would involve moving back into a senior management role. She did not want to do this, because her interest in OD had developed and she wanted to continue working in this area.

Both these major changes would bring about improvements to their quality of life. Nigel's change was internally motivated by a long-held dream of a life in his chosen location following early retirement. Pat's late career move was precipitated by the inflexibility of an organization to enable one of its senior managers to follow the career she wanted. While the career move was externally driven, Pat knew what she wanted to do and her motivation arose from her desire to continue working in her specialist field.

THE CHANGE
EQUATION

Many projects that we initiate are linked to achieving improvements in different aspects of our lives and work. The only difference is the scale and scope of these changes. The 'change equation' below helps us to understand this more clearly:

Change = dissatisfaction + vision + first steps > cost involved

This equation demonstrates that change will not take place until all the individual components have been met. Therefore we need to be dissatisfied with the current situation, have some idea of where we want to go and identify some first steps towards achieving this goal; but we will not change until the sum of all these components is greater than the cost involved.

For Nigel, one of the costs was financial – could he afford his new life? For Pat, two of the costs were leaving the security of an organization in which she had worked for some years and the people whose company she enjoyed.

Case study – Jane

The change equation applies to smaller projects too.

Jane wanted to create more space in her home. It was a small house with two bedrooms and she had insufficient storage space for her clothes (dissatisfaction). She decided to change the use of the small guest bedroom into a dressing room (vision). This involved thinking about how she might create extra storage space and still provide sleeping facilities.

She did some research and found a seat that could be converted into a bed and spoke to a carpenter about designs for built-in storage (first steps). The main cost was financial, so she planned the change when she knew she would have sufficient funds available, and checked with the local estate agent to ensure that converting the bedroom would not reduce the overall value of her property. Having satisfied all four components of the equation, Jane was ready to make the change.

REASONS FOR CHANGE

We make changes in our lives and work for all sorts of reasons. Some common motivators for change are:

boredom with the existing state of affairs

economic factors, such as inheriting money or needing to economize

life transitions, such as mid-life or retirement

finding it difficult to develop, grow or move forward within one's existing situation

external factors, such as children leaving home

excitement about new opportunities that are there for the taking

HOW THIS
BOOK WORKS

Having an idea and initiating change or implementing projects are two different things. Many of us have started projects, only to abandon them halfway through. There are many reasons for this, and these will be explored in this book. The good news is that barriers to change can be overcome, and we can follow a system that will ensure we succeed in making the changes we want to make in our lives through the projects we undertake.

This book has been developed to help you see projects through from start to finish. Whether the project is big or small, the book provides you with a system that can be applied to anything, from decorating a room to changing your job.

Obviously, some projects take longer to implement than others, and some will have further-reaching effects. However, there are some key steps that you can take to maximize the success of any project, large or small. This book aims to introduce you to these steps and provide you with the motivation and confidence to succeed.

SECTION 1 **KNOWING YOURSELF**

Helps you identify your strengths and weaknesses, and develop some knowledge about your capabilities. It also helps you identify the key skills you will need to develop in order to succeed in seeing projects through to their completion.

SECTION 2 **KEY SKILLS FOR ACHIEVING SUCCESS**

Provides expert advice on maximizing your personal strengths and improving the areas of weakness identified in Section 1, through the implementation of ten key skills.

SECTION 3 **10 STAGES TO SUCCESS**

Introduces you to a structured route, in 10 stages, to satisfactorily completing projects, from identifying when you are ready for change to celebrating the successful implementation of the change.

SECTION 4 **PRACTICAL EXERCISES**

Provides some simple practical exercises to assess your understanding of the concepts presented in this book and to provide you with the confidence to get things done.

Section 1
Knowing yourself

This section will help you to analyse and identify your **strengths** and **weaknesses** that can either help or hinder you in achieving what you want, and to establish your 'Personal Portfolio'. You will also learn, through a series of simple exercises, how to develop your knowledge about your own particular capabilities. The text goes on to help you identify the **key skills** you will need to develop in order to succeed in seeing projects through to their completion.

WHAT IS STOPPING YOU ACHIEVING YOUR GOALS?

Having an idea and implementing it are two different things. All of us have strengths and weaknesses that can help us or hold us back in achieving our goals and plans. Some of us believe that we have no willpower and that we will never have the determination to achieve what we want. Others are frightened of failure or lack confidence. Here are some common barriers or pitfalls that can stand in the way of getting things done.

WAITING FOR SOMETHING TO HAPPEN

This can be a multitude of things, such as someone else taking the initiative or the responsibility, winning the lottery or your partner leading the way. The reality is that the longer you wait, the less likely you are to get things done. Yet it is often tempting to put things off by leaving the responsibility to others. Taking responsibility is a key component of implementing projects successfully.

NOT KNOWING WHAT YOU WANT

From our early lives onwards, we are taught about other people's achievements, their ideas, aspirations and challenges. We are rarely encouraged to think about our own achievements, strengths and weaknesses. It can therefore be difficult sometimes to identify what you want and what your priorities are in your life.

HAVE THE RIGHT ATTITUDE!

BE POSITIVE!

HAVE MORE CONFIDENCE!

WHAT DO YOU WANT OUT OF LIFE?

BE DETERMINED!

WHAT MAKES YOU HAPPY?

GET YOURSELF A GOOD CV!

GET YOURSELF ORGANIZED!

THINKING YOU NEED TO TACKLE THE WHOLE PROJECT ALL AT ONCE

Sometimes the sheer size of a project can be daunting and make the task seem just too difficult. Thinking of the project as a large task that cannot be broken down can sometimes put us off getting started, and also makes it harder for us to sustain our motivation because it seems overwhelming. Organizational skills are essential for success.

FAILING TO SET GOALS

Some of us simply like to live for today and have an in-built resistance to setting goals. Goal-setting is crucial to effective project implementation. Research shows that over 90 per cent of people who set goals achieve them.

FEAR OF FAILURE

Some of us develop a false belief that we should be perfect and that failure is a bad thing. In fact, most of us learn best from the things that go least well in our lives. It is the failures that can teach us valuable lessons. Yet we continue to blame ourselves when things don't go well.

COMPARING YOURSELF WITH OTHERS

Many of believe that others are cleverer, better educated, more attractive or nicer than us. This constant comparing process can lower our sense of self-worth and have a negative effect on our self-esteem. How many of us have said 'I would really like to do this, but I'm not good enough'?

FORGETTING TO INVOLVE AND INFLUENCE OTHERS IN MAKING AND IMPLEMENTING OUR PLANS

Some projects, particularly the larger ones, require the assistance, support and co-operation of others. It can be easy to overlook this and to forget to bring in 'key stakeholders' (see page 52) at an early stage.

FAILING TO PRIORITIZE AND MANAGE OUR TIME

'Other things always seem to get in the way!' is a common excuse. It is critical that you prioritize your time to achieve your plans. Otherwise, 'life' can intervene.

NOT HAVING THE NECESSARY SKILLS

We often lack confidence because we don't think that we have the necessary skills to achieve our goals. Sometimes this is true; for example, we may lack assertiveness in particular areas of our lives. In many cases, however, we simply fail to recognize the valuable skills that we do have.

LACK OF WILLPOWER

Having the courage and willpower to achieve what you want is not always easy, particularly when obstacles get in the way. Developing willpower is about maintaining self-discipline and handling the fears that are holding you back.

ANY MORE?

You will surely be able to add to this list when thinking about your own experience of getting things done.

The first step in succeeding in projects and making changes in our lives is to know ourselves, our strengths and weaknesses, our skills and our patterns of behaving in different situations. This is a huge topic and it will take most of us a lifetime to get to know ourselves completely, but there are some key things that are important to know about yourself when implementing projects and making changes.

DEVELOPING
SELF-KNOWLEDGE

The exercises in Section 1 are designed to develop and build on your knowledge about yourself. Be as honest as you can. The exercises may seem a bit daunting at first, so just tackle them in your own time when you are ready. None of the answers are right or wrong, but are aimed at helping you identify how you prefer to behave, and providing you with some insight into how these preferences might affect your motivation and determination to see changes and projects through to the end.

 It is a good idea to start up a 'Personal Portfolio' of your strengths, weaknesses, skills and reflections. Some people find it useful to use a loose-leaf binder to which new pages can be added and others can be removed when they are no longer relevant.

EXERCISE 1
REFLECTION

This exercise can be very encouraging when you are thinking about embarking on a new project. It enables you to reflect on a previous, successful project that you have completed and asks you to ponder some questions that will help you identify what you and others did to ensure the success of the project. The exercise can also help build your confidence by reminding you about the barriers you overcame in achieving your goals. Follow Steps 1 and 2 opposite.

Some of us believe we have no willpower ... others are frightened of failure or lack confidence

Step 1

Think about a project that you have been successful in implementing in the past. Write down the answers to the following questions:

- **What did you do to achieve the successful implementation of the project?**
- **How did you get started?**
- **What skills did you use?**
- **What help did you enlist?**
- **What barriers got in the way and how did you overcome them?**
- **What were the three main things that you did that you believe ensured the project's success?**
- **What were the main feelings you experienced during the project?**
- **What have you learned about your own strengths and weaknesses through undertaking this project?**
- **If you were to undertake a similar project in the future, what would you do differently?**

Step 2

Ask one or two other people who were involved in the project to answer the same questions and to give you some feedback about how they viewed your success. Compare these responses with yours and add to your list of strengths and weaknesses.

EXERCISE 2
YOUR 'PERSONAL JOURNAL'

 Linked to the reflection exercise on the previous page is another method that you can use to enable you to get to know yourself and your responses or reactions to successes and failures. This exercise involves keeping a Personal Journal as part of your Personal Portfolio.

It is not always easy to remember our successes – we tend to focus more on our failures. However, we can also learn from our failures. Use the following method to record significant successes and also events that may not have gone so well. Take a page and divide it into two halves as follows:

WHAT HAPPENED	MY BEHAVIOUR
Note here what happened, who else was involved, what they did and what you think they were feeling and thinking.	*Write down your thoughts and feelings about this event. What did you want to say and do? What did you actually say and do?*

Let a bit of time elapse and then read over your account of the event again. Looking at what happened, how do you feel about it now? What do you think about it? What have you learned from it? What are you going to do now, or in the future?

We can learn from our failures

EXERCISE 3
KNOWING WHAT YOU WANT AND GOAL-SETTING

Human beings tend to fall into two categories: those who think ahead and plan their futures, and those who like to live their lives in a spontaneous way and live mainly for the moment. Both of these positions are valid; however, people who prefer to set goals and plan ahead tend to have more success in implementing projects. Look at the following statements and decide which ones apply to you. This will help you understand which category you fall into.

'Generally, I prefer to plan for tomorrow.'

'I tend to live for today and don't think much about the future.'

'I love change for its own sake.'

'To be happy with change, I need to have a plan.'

'I am clear about what is important for me to focus on in my life and work right now.'

'I know what I would like to be doing in five years' time.'

'I believe that having goals stops me from being spontaneous.'

'It is more important for others to have goals than for me to have them.'

Different methods of goal-setting, to satisfy both personality types, are covered in Section 3 (see page 98). So, even if you prefer to live life for today, it is possible to set goals that meet your preferred ways of operating. Goals need not be restrictive; the secret is to set goals that allow you to be flexible and to make alterations to them if necessary.

WILLPOWER AND MOTIVATION

Willpower and motivation can, on occasion, elude even the most self-disciplined of people. It can be very easy to become distracted, or find that, on certain days, you feel that you want to be doing anything but the tasks you know you should be doing.

Some of us have more staying-power than others. Which of the following statements apply to you?

'I always do my work before I allow myself to play.'

'I can play at any time.'

'I hate to be disturbed when I have settled down to my work.'

'I love interruptions, as they break up my day.'

'I tend to put off till tomorrow what I could do today.'

'I love to see a job right through to the end.'

'I am easily distracted.'

'I can't relax until I've completed my tasks for the day.'

Those of us who are less likely to be distracted or finish their work before going out to play will generally have more 'natural' willpower. However, all of us can learn to minimize distraction and develop willpower whatever our preferences may be.

Set goals that allow you to be flexible

TAKING RESPONSIBILTY FOR YOUR LIFE AND WORK

It can be easy to put things off for all sorts of valid, and not so valid, reasons. The more you procrastinate, however, the more difficult both getting started and completing the project can become.

How many times, when you finally get down to doing something that you have been putting off, do you say to yourself 'Well, that wasn't nearly as difficult as I thought it would be!'?

These exercises can help you identify where you are procrastinating:

WHAT ARE YOU WAITING FOR?

List all the things that you are waiting for. Think of work and other areas of your life. The more areas you identify, the more likely you are to prefer that others take responsibility for them. Notice any patterns that emerge, for example, is there a common theme? This can help you identify areas that you may feel unsure about, lack confidence in or simply don't want to tackle.

WHY ARE YOU WAITING?

Having identified your list and noticed any patterns, ask yourself if you really want to undertake this project and, if yes, why are you procrastinating? Do you need to enlist the help of others, develop some skills or confidence or deal with your feelings of anxiety about the project or change? Being assertively powerful means taking the initiative. Instead of waiting for something to happen, you too can take the first step.

Make some notes in your Personal Portfolio.

FEAR OF FAILURE

One of the main reasons for fear of failure is the belief that you need to get everything 100 per cent right all of the time. Failure means that you are not achieving this state of perfection. The desire to be perfect is normally learned early in our lives. For example, if a child is told often enough by a parent or a teacher that marks of less than 100 per cent are not good enough, they can develop perfectionist patterns and behaviours.

The reality is that, if you are a normal human being, perfection is impossible to achieve. We all make mistakes, and nobody can be right all the time. However, many of us try for that elusive 100 per cent when less would do. Perfectionist patterns can interfere with time management, self-management and building effective relationships, and can also cause us high levels of stress.

ARE YOU A PERFECTIONIST?

Answer the questions below to identify any perfectionist tendencies you may have. Once again, these are not wrong; for example, setting high standards is a good thing, but being too hard on yourself when you fail to meet them can lower your self-esteem. The more questions to which you answered yes, the more likely you are to fear failure and be reluctant to take risks, for example when making changes.

Do you set yourself high standards and then criticize yourself for failing to meet them?

Do you find it hard to make mistakes?

Do you find it hard to aim for less than 100 per cent?

Are you hard on others who fail to meet your standards?

Is it important for you to be right?

HOW DO YOU COPE WITH FAILURE?

This exercise can help you cope with setbacks and failures. Answer the questions as honestly as you can and think about strategies that you might use to deal with failure in the future.

For each question, answer **Often**, **Sometimes** or **Never**.

Section A **Positive reactions**

Do you: see **failure as an inevitable** part of a person's life?

try to **learn from your failures**?

make **contingency plans** in case you fail?

try to **understand why** the answer was no?

maintain good relationships with the people who made the decision, even if you disagree with it?

express your **disappointment** assertively?

use your network to find out why you lost?

maintain your allies so that you can win in the future?

withdraw so that you can **rethink** and try later?

face up to failure and try to turn it around into success in the future?

help others to cope with their disappointment?

support the decision once it's fairly made?

explain to others why the decision was made?

maintain your **positive attitude** in the face of defeat?

If you answer **Often** or **Sometimes** to over half of the questions in section A, you are well on your way to maintaining your power and influence through the way you cope with failure.

If you answer **Often** or **Sometimes** to a high proportion of the questions in section B, you are in danger of letting your failures undermine your power by handling them badly.

Section B **Negative reactions**

Do you: **feel like a failure?**

take it personally?

feel inclined to **play it safe** and not risk failure in the future?

get very angry with the decision-makers, if these were not you?

burn your bridges?

carry on arguing after a firm no?

push and **confront** so that people dig their heels in?

fail to support an unwanted decision when others make the decision?

How did you score?

If you got a high score on section A and a low score on section B, then you are letting your emotions interfere with your ability to be strategic. People do feel passionately about the projects they are involved with. It is therefore natural for them to lose their tempers and their objectivity when they suffer defeat. It is easy to feel rejected, threatened or put down if you fail to get the answer you want. Yet, although passion and anger can be good, they can be destructive if they are not directed into productive channels. Take another look at the points in section A of the questionnaire and see if you can start to use some of these strategies the next time you lose a battle.

Record your insights and strategies in your Personal Portfolio.

IDENTIFYING
YOUR SKILLS

A useful exercise is to think hard about what you do well, rather than always focusing on your failings and consequently undervaluing yourself. You may be surprised at what this reveals.

INVENTORY OF SKILLS AND POSITIVE QUALITIES

Draw up a list of all the things you are good at. Keep going until you have identified 20 or more skills, and then identify the same number of positive qualities that you possess.

Think about your skills in the broadest context. For example, if you are a parent who has chosen to stay at home to look after your children while they are under school age, you might not identify good time management and organizational ability as a particular skill set, but rather as something you have to do to get things done. However, many people believe that these skills are very difficult to develop and they should therefore be valued.

So take the opportunity to do a bit of boasting. List your skills and qualities on a sheet of paper with the following headings and then add them to your Personal Portfolio. It can help you to do this if you involve another person to prompt you and ask questions that will identify all of your valuable skills and qualities.

MY SKILLS – I AM GOOD AT	MY POSITIVE QUALITIES – I AM
1	1
2	2
3	3
4	4
5	5
6	6
7	7
8	8
9	9
10	10
11	11
12	12
13	13
14	14
15	15
16	16
17	17
18	18
19	19
20	20

ASSERTIVENESS AND INFLUENCING SKILLS

Assertiveness is the ability to determine and ask for what you want, set priorities in your life and work and achieve your goals in a positive, direct way, without violating the needs and rights of others. Assertiveness is crucial in helping you to initiate and negotiate within the projects and changes that you want to undertake.

Most of us can be assertive in situations where we feel confident but find it difficult in others. For example, a person might find it very easy to be assertive in meetings at work, but find it harder to be assertive with a friend who asks them to go out on an evening when they would rather stay at home. It is the normal human condition to be assertive in some situations and not in others.

Answer the following questions to help you to assess how assertive you think you are in each of the four different situations:

At work

How do you respond when:

you have to confront a subordinate or colleague for continual lateness, sloppy work or dishonesty?

nosy colleagues interfere in your private affairs?

you notice that someone has worked particularly well or made an extra effort?

you are given unjust criticism?

you are criticized legitimately by a superior?

you feel that your employer persistently demands a lot more of you than you are paid for?

you receive a compliment on your appearance, or someone praises your work?

In public

How do you respond when:

you are confronted with an unhelpful shop assistant?

you take back an article that has been broken or a garment that has shrunk?

the waiter in a restaurant deliberately ignores you?

the food that arrives on your plate is overcooked, cold or bears little resemblance to what you ordered?

you have been waiting ages in a queue and someone barges in front of you?

the doctor dismisses you with a vague comment when you ask for more information?

someone lights up a cigar at the next table just as you are about to start eating?

you are sitting in a library and the person next to you starts talking on their mobile phone?

you suspect you are being sold inferior produce?

Among friends

How do you respond when:

a friend persistently uses you as a shoulder to cry on?

a friend wants to borrow something that you need yourself?

others are putting down something you value highly?

a friend makes what you consider to be an unreasonable request?

someone is making nasty remarks about a person who is important to you?

you have to negotiate with a friend about which film to see or where to meet?

you want to ask for the repayment of a loan of some money?

you are upset by a racist or sexist comment?

you feel put down or disregarded by a friend?

At home

How do you respond when:

you want some privacy at home?

you want to say yes to an invitation, but your partner has other plans for you?

you want to say no to a child's request?

everyone leaves the cleaning or washing-up to you?

you want to say no to a proposed visit of a relative?

one of your parents criticizes you?

Select an example from each of the above four categories that you think you handle less well than you would like to. Identify how you think you behave in these situations.

Ask yourself the following questions:

'What am I saying and doing in these situations?'
'How do I feel about my behaviour in these situations?'
'What are my short-term gains or pay-offs for behaving in this way?'
'How do I think my behaviour is affecting the other person?'
'What are the long-term negative effects of this behaviour, on others and myself?'

Then select an example that you think you generally handle well.

Ask yourself these questions:

'What am I saying or doing that I am pleased about in dealing with these situations?'
'What are the risks involved in behaving in this way?'
'How do I think my behaviour is affecting the other person?'
'What are the long-term benefits of this behaviour, on others and myself?'

After you have carried out the analysis, make some notes in your Personal Portfolio of what you have learned about your behaviour in different situations. For example, are there any patterns emerging? Do you want to be more assertive? Do you over-use any types of behaviour that serve you less well? The behaviours will be defined in more detail in Section 2.

Focus on what you do well

PRIORITIZING AND MANAGING
YOUR TIME

The ability to plan, organize and manage time is a crucial element of project management and implementation. These skills can be learned, but many people find them difficult to do well. Our relationship with time will have a direct impact on how we manage our projects and changes.

Answer the series of questions below to help you to assess your time-management skills.

Do you: **tackle the most difficult tasks early in the morning?**

write a list of 'Things that must be done today'?

ever say no when asked to do something?

ever ask why when invited to go to a meeting?

think that other people waste less time than you do?

give priority to matters that are urgent, rather than to those that are important?

put all tasks into priority order and work on them in that order?

tackle one task at a time, finish it and then move on to the next one?

accept all unscheduled interruptions?

prefer doing things yourself rather than give them to others to do?

ask other people how they organize their time?

NEXT STEPS

Now you are in a position of strength, having assessed your current skills, strengths and weaknesses. Review your responses to the above questions and exercises and ask yourself: 'What does this tell me about myself?'

Add your findings to your Personal Portfolio. Discuss these with some people who are close to you, for example a work colleague, a friend or a family member. Encourage them to give you feedback and their personal observations.

It can be easy for us to focus on our weaknesses rather than our strengths. Remember that it is your strengths that will help you the most to succeed in the projects and changes that you want to achieve. So these are as important as your weaknesses.

Sections 2 and 3 of this book will help you build on your strengths, eliminate or improve your weaknesses and develop your skills. Section 4 sets out some useful exercises to help you check your understanding and gain the confidence to apply your skills.

Your strengths will help you to succeed

Section 2
Key skills for achieving success

Section 1 helped you assess your **strengths** and **skills**, and identify areas you want to improve.

This section provides you with expert help in developing those weaknesses that you think might be holding you back from implementing the projects and changes that you would like to achieve.

Ten key skills are highlighted to form a **'Resource Pack'** that will help you make the changes you want. Some general exercises are contained in this section to help you work through the theory in a practical way.

SKILL 1
HOW TO FIND MOTIVATION AND WILLPOWER

The first step to success is really to want the project to happen and to have sufficient motivational factors in place to make the effort worthwhile.

Case study

Ernie wanted to give up smoking, and he had made several unsuccessful attempts in the past. He was asthmatic and knew that his smoking was damaging his health. He used to get bronchitis every winter. However, his enjoyment of smoking was greater than his motivation to stop.

Then two significant things changed. Ernie met a new partner who did not smoke and did not like others smoking. His doctor, who was also a personal friend, told him that if Ernie came into his surgery next winter with bronchitis, he would refuse to treat him!

These additional motivational factors were what Ernie needed to provide him with some extra encouragement, and he succeeded in stopping smoking within six months.

The key to finding willpower is to really want things to change. Without the desire, the willpower will be hard to find. By applying the change equation described in the Introduction (see page 8) to your situation or project, you can measure your will to change and the motivation to succeed. If the will is not there, then it is better not to embark on the project at all. This is not a sign of failure, but an honest acknowledgement that it may not be right to make the change at the present time.

For some of us, finding additional motivational factors is not the cure for our lack of motivation or willpower. We can be really keen to make a change, but for some reason we just can't muster enough motivation to get started, or we find ourselves losing enthusiasm as the project goes on. Improving courage and willpower is like developing muscles – the more you use them the stronger they become. Then it can simply be a question of practising some simple exercises to help you to develop your willpower so that you manage to sustain your interest and motivation.

WILL-POWER

Here are some exercises that can help you improve your willpower. They divide into two categories, some that require an effort of will actually to do, and others where the act is quite easy but the will comes in trying to do them every day. Select the exercises that you think will work best for you.

The first step to success is really to want the project to happen

EXERCISES THAT NEED EFFORT

When you are tempted to say something, **hold back and don't say it.**

When you want to do something immediately, don't.
Postpone it instead to a definite, specified time in the future.

When you want to postpone something, don't. **Do it right away.**

Do something that you know you don't want to do. This could be something simple like walking to the shops rather than taking the car.

Do something that you have never tried before, such as sampling a new type of dish that you think you won't like when you are in a restaurant.

Talk to a complete stranger each day.

Think of a situation that you would normally avoid, for example making a complaint about poor service, and then do it.

EXERCISES THAT NEED REPETITION EACH DAY

Do these at the same time each day.

Go for a short walk.

    Read a newspaper.

        Deal with the mail.

           Clean one of the rooms in the house.

           Check your e-mails.

These exercises can be a great help in developing your ability to apply yourself to tasks that require self-discipline and courage.

SKILL 2
DEALING WITH YOUR NEGATIVE INNER VOICE

Another factor that can prevent us from finding the motivation to succeed in our projects is the negative inner voice that can suddenly leap into our thoughts. This voice normally appears when we are feeling vulnerable or when we are facing a particularly difficult challenge. The negative voice can be the result of beliefs we have come to accept about ourselves. We tend to be judged in society largely according to how we measure up to the relevant norms.

When compared to their peers, children may be exceptional at athletics, average at reading or poor at mathematics. Adults constantly make comparisons about all aspects of the behaviour of children – their intelligence, beauty, manners, work habits, ability to play with other children and so on. In addition, adults often label children as, for example, loving or spiteful, friendly or mean, reasonable or selfish, co-operative or unco-operative, outgoing or shy. As we mature, these comparisons and labels are applied to all of us, first by adults, increasingly by our peers and eventually by ourselves.

NEGATIVE COMPARISONS

Having internalized the standards and beliefs of those who judge us, we gradually come to describe ourselves in terms of how we deviate from the norm. For example, we may say to ourselves 'I may look pretty but I'm not clever'. Listening to these negative messages can erode our confidence and lower our self-esteem.

Here are some more examples of negative and counter-productive talk that can speak to us.

Self-punishment – 'What a stupid thing to do, you fool.'
Negative self-labelling – 'I'm mean, lazy, unattractive' and so on.
Self-pressurizing – 'I must', 'I've got to', 'I ought', 'I should'.
Making assumptions – 'People won't like me if ...'
Magnifying – 'This is so difficult, I can't possibly handle it.'
Catastrophizing – 'If I don't ask the right questions, they won't be impressed and I won't get the job.'
Believing there is no choice – 'It's success or failure.'

ARRESTING THE INNER SABOTEUR

It is really useful to recognize these negative messages for what they are – inappropriate, irrational and unreasonable. By becoming aware of them, you will begin to understand how you can block your own ability to succeed.

The next time you hear your negative inner voice, challenge it – is it really saying something valid and reasonable? Try replacing negative messages with positive, supportive ones. This process of challenge can provide you with a more accurate self-concept and help raise your self-esteem.

'It's OK to make mistakes.'

'I'm not stupid, although that was not the best decision I've ever made.'

'I'm not lazy, just taking time to think about how to proceed.'

DEVELOPING SELF-ENHANCING THOUGHTS

Think for a moment and list three to five good personal attributes of yourself or your life such as positive beliefs about your appearance, intelligence, range of interests or life achievements (if necessary, return to the list of positive qualities you identified in Section 1 to help you). These should be truthful and concrete, such as 'I have a nice smile' or 'I am well informed about current affairs'.

Now aim to increase how often you recall these self-enhancing thoughts. You can do this by following each positive self-statement with an immediate reward. Many everyday activities qualify as rewards – eating, drinking, playing a game, phoning a friend and so on. Repeat a few of your self-enhancing statements just before the rewarding activity; in this way you reward yourself for thinking positive thoughts and so these thoughts are strengthened by the pleasurable act that follows.

Carry your list of positive messages with you wherever you go. Take them out and read them when you are feeling down or lacking in confidence.

Achievements and positive qualities:

'I am friendly'

'I have a degree'

'I can handle my drink'

TAKING RISKS

At any time during your project, you may be faced with making a decision or undertaking a task that feels risky. You may, for example, need to ask your boss for a big favour, or make a decision that you know will displease a friend. Taking risks is an important part of making changes and implementing projects. To take risks, however, we need to confront our fears.

STEPPING OUT OF THE COMFORT ZONE

Our 'comfort zone' is the area of our lives and work within which we can operate with comfort on a day-to-day basis. We feel that we are in control and can handle with ease any situation that comes our way. Working within our personal comfort zone enables us to operate with confidence and maximizes our likelihood of success.

COMFORT ZONE
- Day-to-day routine
- Familiar environment
- Friends and family
- An easy life

OPPORTUNITY

CHALLENGE

RISK

FEAR

CHANGE

However, certain situations arise that can threaten to take us outside our comfort zone, such as a new opportunity or a very challenging one. Our natural reaction is often to retreat into our comfort zone and bury our head in the sand in the vain hope that the situation will somehow disappear. We know that if we are to deal with the situation, this will mean taking a risk, with all of the associated fears inherent in that risk.

Our negative inner voice begins to take over, and we start to catastrophize about what will happen if we step outside our comfort zone. Yet, to develop and move forward, to achieve change and to be successful, we know deep down that we need to stretch the boundaries of our comfort zone outwards, otherwise it will start shrinking in on us.

How many times have you felt fearful about something and, when you plucked up the courage to confront it, the fear recedes and the situation seems less of a problem than you thought? Research has shown that approximately four out of five fears never materialize. Of the ones that do materialize, however, we often find that we can handle them anyway, because, as human beings, we are much more resilient and resourceful than we give ourselves credit for.

Therefore, when you are making changes or undertaking projects, it is useful to notice the types of fears you are experiencing that might stop you taking the risks that you know you need to take if the change is going to happen.

This is not about being reckless, but about analysing your fears and challenging your negative inner voice that might be preventing you from moving forward. Then it is about trusting your good judgement and repeating to yourself your internal mantra: 'Just do it.'

Four out of five fears never materialize

Case study

As mentioned on page 7, Nigel was planning for his retirement. While doing this, he experienced lots of fears, including:

being bored, without his day-to-day routine of travelling to the office

alienating his wife, who initially did not want to uproot and leave the city

having insufficient money to live on

leaving his friends and family behind

failing to achieve his dream

discovering he had made a mistake in moving

He managed his fears by examining them and building strategies into his project plan to minimize and neutralize them, such as adjusting his plan to make savings when the stock market was giving him lower returns on his investments. By taking charge of his fears, he felt more in control of them and more able to move forward.

MANAGING YOUR FEARS

It is not always possible to reduce all your fears. It is acceptable, however, to feel fear, since at the other end of the scale lies excitement. Excitement is a positive feeling and an essential one to experience when making changes. Here are some strategies for managing your fears so that they don't get in the way of your success.

Strategies

- Talk about your fears to friends and family; seek and listen to their encouragement.
- Practise taking small risks first, and notice the feelings of satisfaction and achievement associated with them.
- Gradually increase the level of risks you take.
- Use affirmations to challenge your negative inner voice, for example by repeating to yourself how well you are performing a particular task, if your fear is that you will fail in achieving it.
- Allow yourself to feel fear; it is a valuable indicator that you are on the brink of a change. But then try instead to get in touch with the excitement that the change will bring when you have achieved it.

Handling your fear is an essential skill to draw upon when you are undertaking change. Many of us fear change and, if we allow our fear to control us, we can lose sight of the reasons why we have decided to make the change in the first place. It is not always easy for us to handle our fear, and our first instinct is often to run away from it. Remember, however, that you don't have to deal with your fear on your own, and that if you do confront your fears, they will often disappear.

We need to stretch the boundaries of our comfort zone

SKILL 3
ASSERTIVENESS
FOR INFLUENCE

There are many situations where assertiveness can help you to succeed with your projects and changes. Here the focus is on two key areas:

1 Taking the initiative, remaining positive and setting goals.
2 Identifying and influencing your 'stakeholders'.

TAKING THE INITIATIVE, REMAINING POSITIVE AND SETTING GOALS

Assertiveness is one of the behaviours that we can choose to use when dealing with other people. It is also a state of mind that reflects our attitudes, beliefs, values and self-esteem.

If we imagine an onion cut down through the middle, the behaviour is the visible skin, the outer layer. Underneath the onion skin, however, there are other layers which represent the different components of our personalities and which will affect our behaviour. These include our inner thoughts and feelings, our attitudes and beliefs, and our values. Right in the centre of the onion is our self-esteem, which also plays a key role in how we behave.

BEHAVIOUR

THOUGHTS
AND FEELINGS

ATTITUDES

BELIEFS

VALUES

SELF-
ESTEEM

We have four behaviour options to choose from when it comes to dealing with other people:

1 BEING ASSERTIVE	3 BEING PASSIVE
2 BEING AGGRESSIVE	4 USING INDIRECT AGGRESSION OR MANIPULATIVE BEHAVIOUR

1 Being assertive

Assertive behaviour involves a genuine respect for the people we deal with. As we are increasingly able to accept our positive and negative personal characteristics, we become more able to accept others. We don't need to put others down because we don't feel the need to win. Instead of believing that others are responsible for our lives, we can accept responsibility for our choices and behaviours.

We can acknowledge our needs and ask openly and directly, even though in doing so we risk refusal and possible rejection. If refused and rejected, we are not totally demolished because our self-esteem is anchored deeply within ourselves, and is not dependent on the approval of others. We can learn to set limits assertively so that others know where they stand with us. We can respond sincerely to others and cope with situations appropriately, giving ourselves credit for what we understand and feel.

Assertive behaviour means taking a positive and pro-active approach

It is rooted in high self-esteem and it is the behaviour that is the most likely to get us the results that we are looking for, although it does not guarantee that you will always get what you want. Assertiveness is about compromise and negotiating a win-win outcome. It is not always easy to use.

2 Being aggressive

Aggressive behaviour is competitive, and the implicit or explicit goal is to emerge as the winner. Therefore, someone has to lose. This is usually achieved by putting others down or over-riding their feelings, wishes or rights. With very little real self-esteem, the aggressive person cannot afford to consider another person's point of view; so, when faced with a conflict or confrontation, the aggressive character responds with outright attack.

Aggression results in compulsive over-reaction; we resort to verbal or even physical abuse, leaving behind a trail of hurt or humiliated feelings. These feelings may never be expressed directly through fear of provoking another onslaught, but past actions continue to harbour feelings of resentment in others.

3 Being passive

Passive behaviour is characterized by being the 'doormat', and makes ideal fodder for the aggressive tactics of the character described above. The passive type believes that they are a victim of unfairness and injustice at the hands of other people, or maybe fate. Decisions are impossible – it is easier to opt out and allow others to make decisions. Others will often resent this characteristic passivity. They may begin by wanting to help, but then feel guilty and perplexed because whatever they do, it is never enough. The hard-luck stories begin to lose their conviction as would-be helpers lose patience and try to avoid contact.

The passive outlook is negative and results in the person feeling frustrated by their lack of willpower and adopting an attitude of profound resignation. There is a constant theme of self-negation and self-pity, and the prospect of confrontation provokes immediate acquiescence or avoidance by running away.

4 Using indirect aggression or manipulative behaviour

Indirect aggressive behaviour also arises from low self-esteem. Instead of the more obvious aggressive tactics, indirect behaviour is more subtle and hidden. The need to manipulate stems from fear of exposure – it becomes safer to control and manipulate than face confrontation and risk being rejected.

Manipulation involves deceiving ourselves and others, and getting our needs met by the devious means of making others feel guilty if they don't do what we want. On the surface, the indirectly aggressive or manipulative character may appear to think highly of others, but an undercurrent of disapproval can often be detected. However, any attempt to probe or clarify is met with denial, so that people are left feeling puzzled, thwarted and guilty.

Passive behaviour makes ideal fodder for the aggressive

CHANGING BEHAVIOUR

Although we all use all of the behaviours described above, we can sometimes develop patterns of behaviour in particular situations or with particular individuals. Because we learn our behaviour from an early age, these patterns can become well-established, even if they may not always serve us well. The good news is that as we learn our behaviour, we can change it if we think we need to. While changing our behaviour is not always easy, with determination and a little willpower we can succeed.

When embarking on projects or changes, it can be useful to identify your preferred patterns of behaviour in particular situations, as these will have a positive or negative impact on how you approach your projects and influence their success.

Case study

As mentioned on page 7, Pat had decided to change her job. One of the first steps she took was to ask the Director of Human Resources (HR) if she could work flexible hours and undertake commissions for external clients in her free time. She felt very apprehensive about making this request, and her negative inner voice went into overdrive, bombarding her with messages that she was just not good enough to be even contemplating freelance work as an organizational development consultant.

This was causing her to behave in a passive way. She cancelled her appointment with the Director of HR three times. She then asked a friend for support, and her friend gave her lots of compliments about her skills and encouraged her to make a further appointment. She recommended that Pat thought very clearly about what she wanted and where she might compromise, if she was unable to achieve her ideal outcome. She also encouraged Pat to rehearse what she was going to say so that she would sound confident and positive at the meeting.

Pat went to the meeting, still a little apprehensive, but with more confidence in her ability and also her right to ask for what she wanted. Her request was granted immediately. In fact, the Director of HR said that he was delighted that Pat had taken charge of her own career and that, if she needed any further assistance, she should make a point of seeing him again. Pat was delighted and, to assist her with future situations where she found behaving in an assertive way difficult, she enrolled on an assertiveness course.

STEPS TO ASSERTIVENESS

By being: **a) clear about what she wanted,**
b) feeling positive about her intentions and
c) taking the initiative.

By taking control Pat achieved a significant first step in moving towards her new career as a freelance consultant. She also practised what she wanted to say so that she was in the best position to influence the other person, a more senior figure in her organization.

This was not an easy step for Pat to take, however, and she had to be careful not to revert to her preferred behaviour in this situation – passive behaviour – which would have stopped her from achieving what she wanted.

Being assertive means planning and preparing what you want to say. It can seem time-consuming but, as you can see from Pat's example, it can also reap rewards.

Take control and reap the rewards

IDENTIFYING AND INFLUENCING YOUR 'STAKEHOLDERS'

With larger projects such as moving house or restructuring a department, some people will have a key role to play, and may present a barrier to the successful completion of the project. It is important to identify all the key people, or 'stakeholders', whom you will need to influence if the project is going to be successful. Stakeholders can be people who will be directly involved in your project, such as your family, or simply people you need to influence to make it happen. The diagram below illustrates some of the stakeholders involved in a plan to move house.

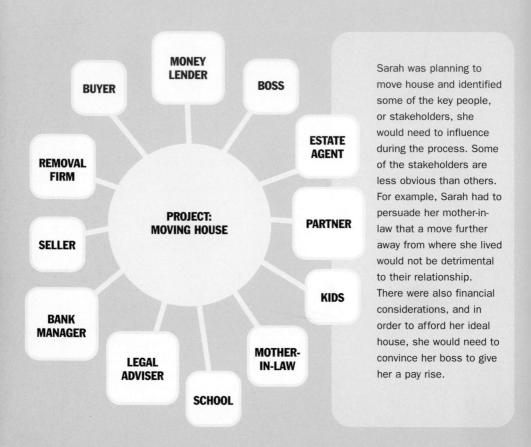

MONEY LENDER

BUYER

BOSS

ESTATE AGENT

REMOVAL FIRM

PROJECT: MOVING HOUSE

PARTNER

SELLER

KIDS

BANK MANAGER

LEGAL ADVISER

MOTHER-IN-LAW

SCHOOL

Sarah was planning to move house and identified some of the key people, or stakeholders, she would need to influence during the process. Some of the stakeholders are less obvious than others. For example, Sarah had to persuade her mother-in-law that a move further away from where she lived would not be detrimental to their relationship. There were also financial considerations, and in order to afford her ideal house, she would need to convince her boss to give her a pay rise.

PREPARING TO MEET THE BOSS

Identify your stakeholders, then influence them. Some will be straightforward, others may be more of an unknown quantity. For example, Sarah will have a good idea of her partner's view, but she may not be so sure of her boss's response to a request for a pay rise. It would therefore be useful to do some research before she meets her boss so that she is fully prepared feels confident.

THE MEETING MODEL

Many people will find the following model useful. Ask yourself these questions before meeting with any of your stakeholders.

YOURSELF	*What are your strengths and weaknesses?* *What influence do you have?* *How do you feel about your relationship?* *How might you prepare for the meeting?*
STAKEHOLDERS	*What are their strengths and weaknesses?* *What might their position be?* *How much power do they have to grant your request?* *How do they view your relationship with them?*
THE TASK	*What is your objective?* *Where might you compromise?* *What is your ideal outcome?* *What might you expect realistically and what is your bottom line or fallback position?* *What resources might you need?* *What are the constraints?*
THE ENVIRONMENT	*Where is the best place to hold a meeting?* *What sort of atmosphere do you want to create – formal or informal?* *When would be the best time?* *Will you be free from interruptions?*

Assertive behaviour will normally bring you the most effective results in influencing others, because it is the behaviour that it is most useful to apply when you want to develop and sustain relationships.

Case study

Let's take Jane's room change (see page 9). One of the people she needed to influence was her partner, Richard. He thought that changing the bedroom to a dressing room would be counter-productive and would reduce the value of the property. He could also see no point in employing a carpenter, as he could build the new wardrobes himself.

Richard's position posed two main problems for Jane that she needed to address and overcome.

- **How could she convince Richard that transforming the bedroom was a good idea?**

- **How could she convince Richard to employ a carpenter (she had witnessed Richard's attempts at carpentry before)?**

Jane did her homework and spoke to the bank about the possibility of the change reducing the value of the property. The bank confirmed that the room change was more likely to add value to the property, as it provided more storage and you could still fit a single bed into the room. She presented the figures to Richard and proposed that they go ahead with the change as planned. Richard agreed. The second scenario was not so easy. Richard found it hard to understand why Jane wanted to employ a carpenter when he could just as easily build the wardrobes.

FIVE ASSERTIVE SKILLS

These can be used in a variety of situations and provide a structure within which to work. They are not presented in any particular order, but it is worth spending time on working out what specifically you want to say, as this is often enough to influence the other person.

1 Being specific

This involves deciding what it is you want or feel and being prepared to say so specifically and directly. It involves keeping your statement simple and brief. For example, the most direct way to refuse a request is to say no. However, we often use other options, which are at best watered down and at worst confusing.

2 Repetition

Sometimes referred to as the 'broken record technique', this skill helps you to stay with your statement or request by using a calm repetition. Using this technique, you can maintain a steady position without falling prey to manipulative comments, irrelevant logic or argumentative bait, designed to take you away from your point.

3 Dealing with manipulation

This is also known as the 'fogging technique' or 'fielding the response'. In order to communicate most effectively when others are trying to manipulate you, indicate that you have heard what the other person says, but without getting 'hooked' by what they say and straying away from your point. This skill allows you to acknowledge the other person's response and still continue confidently with your statement or request, instead of feeling defensive or aggressive.

4 Workable compromise

It is important to remember that when there is a conflict between your needs and wishes and those of someone else, assertiveness is not about winning at the expense of the other person. So you need to negotiate from an equal position. This means finding a true compromise that takes both parties' needs into consideration.

Compromising on a solution to a difficult situation need not mean compromising your self-respect. In any situation where you are preparing to be assertive, it is useful to identify what your ideal outcome would be, what your realistic position might be and what constitutes your fallback position or bottom line.

5 Self-disclosure

This skill allows you to disclose your feelings with a simple statement, such as 'I feel nervous' or 'I feel guilty'. The immediate effect is to reduce your anxiety or guilt, thus enabling you to relax and take charge of yourself and your feelings.

Jane used the 'Five assertive skills' to help her in the dialogue that took place between her and Richard.

Richard, I'd really like to employ Tony (the carpenter) to build the wardrobes in the dressing room.
(*Being specific*)

It's OK, as I said before, I can build the wardrobes.

Richard, I'm feeling anxious about saying this, but I would like Tony to build the wardrobes as I think he'd do a more professional and quicker job. (*Repetition and self-disclosure*)

I thought that you believed I was good at DIY.

I do think that you are great at some DIY projects, but I don't think carpentry is one of your strong points and I think we should ask Tony to build the wardrobes. (*Fielding the response*) How about we compromise and Tony builds them and you paint them? (*Workable compromise*)

Well, if you really don't think I could do them properly...

It's not that I think you couldn't do them properly, it's just that Tony is a skilled carpenter who has been trained to build wardrobes (*Fielding the response*) and that he will produce excellent results in a shorter time.

Oh, all right then, but let's see if we can get him to reduce his price a bit.

All five assertive skills were used in the dialogue between Richard and Jane. By remaining calm, clear and honest, Jane was able to influence Richard to employ Tony. Jane also chose the right time to approach Richard; she raised the subject when they had the time to discuss it, over a meal.

Being assertive is not always easy, and it can take a lot of time and energy. However, it is the only behaviour that will build your self-esteem and provide you with the best opportunity to influence others successfully. Therefore, in the long term, the extra effort required will usually be worth it.

Assertiveness is about compromise and negotiating a win-win outcome

SKILL 4
HANDLING CONFLICT

The dialogue between Jane and Richard (see pages 56–57) presented several opportunities for conflict to arise. The definition of conflict in this situation was when there was a difference in position, or point of view, between two parties that could not be resolved. It was through using assertive behaviour, which enabled Jane to remain calm and in control, that she enabled conflict to be avoided.

However, the dialogue could have gone very differently, had Jane used different behaviours.

Richard, I'd really like to employ Tony (the carpenter) to build the wardrobes in the dressing room.

It's OK, as I said before, I can build the wardrobes.

The trouble with you, Richard, is that you think you're an expert in DIY, but you're totally useless at it.

I'm not useless at DIY.

Yes, you are. There are a whole host of unfinished projects and botched jobs around the house and I'm really sick of it!

Getting Tony in would be a complete waste of money and I won't hear of it – I'll build the wardrobes.

Over my dead body!

As usual, you have to have the last word!

Many of us will be familiar with such aggressive dialogue. A probable outcome is that the issue will remain unresolved, with the likelihood that Richard will go ahead and build the wardrobes without Jane's agreement, while they become further entrenched in their positions, both thinking they are right.

RESOLVING CONFLICT

Conflict situations are those in which the concerns of two parties appear to be incompatible. In such situations, a person's behaviour falls into two basic types: **confrontation** (the extent to which the individual attempts to satisfy their own concerns) and **co-operation** (the extent to which the individual attempts to satisfy the other person's concerns).

Five approaches to resolving conflicts have been identified:

1 COMPETING   4 COLLABORATING
2 ACCOMMODATING   5 COMPROMISING
3 AVOIDING

All these approaches are useful and can be employed in different situations when conflicts arise. The skill is being able to select the correct approach for resolving each particular conflict. The two behaviour types described above can be used to define these five specific methods of dealing with conflicts.

1 Competing

This approach is confrontational and unco-operative. It is where an individual pursues their own concerns at the expense of those of the other person. This is a power-orientated style in which someone uses whatever power seems appropriate – their ability to argue, their rank, economic sanction – to gain the upper hand. Competing might mean standing up for your rights, defending a position that you believe is correct or simply trying to win.

2 Accommodating

This approach is non-confrontational and co-operative – the opposite of competing. When accommodating, an individual neglects their own concerns to satisfy the concerns of others; there is an element of self sacrifice in this style. Accommodating might take the form of selfless generosity of charity, obeying another person's order when you would prefer not to or yielding to another's point of view.

3 Avoiding

This approach is non-confrontational and unco-operative. The individual does not immediately pursue their own concerns or those of the other person. This approach does not address the conflict. Avoiding might take the form of diplomatically sidestepping an issue, postponing an issue until a better time or simply withdrawing from a threatening situation.

4 Collaborating

This approach is both confrontational and co-operative – the opposite of avoiding. Collaborating involves an attempt to work with the other person to find some solution that fully satisfies the concerns of both parties. It means digging into an issue to identify the underlying concerns of the two individuals and to find a solution that meets both sets of concerns. Collaborating between two parties might take the form of: exploring a disagreement to learn from each other's insights; agreeing to resolve some condition that would otherwise have them competing for resources; or confronting and trying to find a creative solution to an interpersonal problem.

5 Compromising

This approach is intermediate in both confrontation and co-operation. The objective is to find some expedient, mutually acceptable solution that partially satisfies both parties. It falls on a middle ground between competing and accommodating. Compromising gives up more than competing but less than accommodating. Likewise, it addresses an issue more directly than avoiding, but doesn't explore it in as much depth as collaborating. Compromising might mean splitting the difference, exchanging concessions or seeking a quick middle-ground position.

SELECTING THE APPROPRIATE CONFLICT-HANDLING STYLE

The different approaches to resolving conflicts might be applied in the following situations.

Competing

When **quick, decisive action** is vital, e.g. emergencies.

On important issues when **unpopular courses of action need implementing**, e.g. cost-cutting, enforcing unpopular rules, discipline.

On issues vital to company welfare **when you know you are right**.

To **protect yourself** against people who take advantage of non-competitive behaviour.

Accommodating

When **you realize that you are wrong** – to allow a better position to be heard, to learn from others and to show that you are reasonable.

When **the issue is much more important to the other person than to yourself** – to satisfy the needs of others, and as a goodwill gesture to help maintain a co-operative relationship.

To **build up social credits** for later issues which are important to you.

When continued competing would only **damage your cause**, where you are outmatched and losing.

When **preserving harmony and avoiding disruption** are especially important.

To **aid in the managerial development** of others by letting them experiment and learn from their own mistakes.

Avoiding

When **an issue is trivial,** of only passing importance or when other more important issues are pressing.

When you perceive **no chance of satisfying your concerns**, e.g. when you have low power or you are frustrated by something that would be very difficult to change (national policies, someone's personality, structure, etc.).

When the potential **damage of confronting a conflict** outweighs the benefits of its resolution.

To **let people cool down** – to reduce tensions to a productive level and to regain perspective and composure.

When **gathering more information** outweighs the advantages of an immediate decision.

When **others can resolve the conflict** more effectively.

When the **issue seems tangential** or symptomatic of another more basic issue.

Collaborating

To **find an integrative solution** when both sets of concerns are too important to be compromised.

When your objective is to learn, e.g. **testing your own assumptions**, understanding the views of others.

To **merge insights from other people** with different perspectives on a problem.

To gain commitment by **incorporating others' concerns** into a consensual decision.

Teamwork through hard feelings that have been interfering with an interpersonal relationship.

Compromising

When **goals are moderately important**, but not worth the effort or potential disruption of more confrontational styles.

When two opponents with equal power are strongly committed to **mutually exclusive goals**, e.g. in labour-management bargaining.

To achieve **temporary settlements** to complex issues.

To arrive at **expedient solutions** under time pressure.

As a back-up style when **collaborating or competing fails** to be successful.

EXERCISE IN CONFLICT ASSESSMENT

You can identify the appropriate style to apply to a real-life conflict, based on two key considerations:

- **the importance of the outcome.**
- **the importance of the relationship with the other person involved in the conflict.**

Below are ten pairs of statements. Each pair describes a conflict situation. In each case, circle the letter of the one statement that you think fits your conflict situation better.

P *I don't really care what the other person thinks of me when the conflict is over.*
R *It is important I have a good relationship with the person once the conflict is over.*

M *It won't be the end of the world if I don't resolve this conflict.*
O *I have vital interests at stake in resolving this conflict.*

P *I don't have a significant personal or business relationship with the other person.*
R *My relationship with the other person is important for business or personal reasons.*

M *The time and trouble needed to resolve this conflict might not be worth it.*
O *I expect the resolution of this conflict to be worth my while if it goes reasonably well.*

P *There is very little sharing of feelings and information.*
R *My relationship with the other person is based on shared feelings and information.*

M *I don't expect resolving this conflict to affect future dealings with the other person.*
O *Resolving this conflict will set the pattern for many future conflicts.*

P *My communication with the other person has been quite limited.*
R *My communication with the other person has been extensive.*

M *I will not feel any worse about myself if I end up thinking I lost the conflict.*
O *I won't feel really good unless I do well in this conflict.*

P *I am not dependent on the other person.*
R *We have common interests because of the ways in which we are thrown together.*

M *The issues at stake here are clear and straightforward.*
O *I suspect there are important hidden factors at stake in this conflict.*

Scoring

Count your letter scores. How many Rs did you circle? How many Os did you circle? Your responses can now be plotted on the model below, to assist you to identify the strategy that might be the most useful for you in resolving the conflict.

SKILL 5
CONFRONTATION

A method of getting the other person to move when all else fails is confrontation. This, when skilfully used, is a very powerful influence or conflict-handling style, but it should only be used sparingly. People who are seen as very confrontational tend to be feared and avoided.

WHAT IS CONFRONTATION?

Confrontation is making explicit the difference between:

- **what you value and what the other person values.**
- **what you think and what the other person thinks.**
- **what you feel and what the other person feels.**

When you do this, you risk hurting the other person's feelings.

Confrontation also makes differences explicit between:

- **what you want to do and what the other person wants to do.**
- **what you actually do and what the other person actually does.**

When you do this, somebody has to change their behaviour; the risk is that it may be you.

Confrontation also makes differences explicit between what the other person says and what they do. When you do this, you risk making the other person angry (defensive).

Conflict is inevitable

HOW TO CONFRONT

1. Acknowledge the other person's position as legitimate (for them).
2. Differentiate the other person's position from yours.
3. Check to see whether you have heard the other person clearly and that they have heard you.
4. Accept angry, hostile feelings in yourself and in the other person as real. Be responsible for your own feelings. Leave the other person free to feel differently.
5. Don't try to solve the problem until differences have been fully explained.
6. Ask the other person to describe their preferred solution. Be prepared to state (and differentiate) yours.

USING CONFRONTATIONAL STATEMENTS CONSTRUCTIVELY

The following statements are confrontational, but not aggressive, meaning that they can be used in a constructive manner to try to resolve conflict situations.

SKILL 6
MANAGING ANGER AND FRUSTRATION ASSERTIVELY

Conflict situations often cause us to feel angry or frustrated. If we allow our feelings of anger or frustration to build up, we can lose control of a situation and find it difficult to remain assertive. Below are some strategies for effectively handling and channelling your anger when conflicts arise.

RECOGNITION

The first step in managing your anger and frustration is to recognize it. Learn to identify the signals that you are angry. For example, what are the physical symptoms that you display when you become angry, or how do you behave? It can also be useful to notice the ways you have of denying your anger.

DECISION

Then decide what to do with it. Mark it 'for attention' and take some time to look at it, either immediately or later. Generally, it is not productive to express your anger to another person until you feel in control of your emotions. If you think you need more time to calm down, take yourself away from the situation until you have regained your composure. The 'avoiding' approach to conflict-handling can be a very useful strategy here.

USE

Employ your anger as an energy source, using it constructively to power ideas and projects, and to make changes.

EXPRESSION

Give your anger a safe form of physical expression (later and/or in private, as appropriate). Strategies might include physical exercise, such as swimming, running, shouting, tearing (unwanted) papers or even tackling that clearing-out job you have been putting off.

VOICING

Use the assertive skill of self-disclosure to voice your anger. Be sure to 'own' your anger. Avoid saying 'you make me angry'. Just say, simply, 'I'm angry'. Be honest when you voice your anger and be careful not to downgrade it by, for example, saying 'I'm a bit annoyed' when in fact you are feeling furious. Also try to avoid modifying it by describing your anger as another feeling, such as 'I'm upset' or 'I'm unhappy'. Treat your anger seriously, not lightly.

KNOWLEDGE

Get to know your anger. Discover its range: for example, from mild irritation to raging fury. It can be helpful to catch it in its milder forms, and voice it then, rather than letting it develop further. Your anger is a life-saving signal, so respect it and make friends with it. It is important when dealing with conflicts to separate present anger from past anger. In some situations, and with some people, we can develop what is called 'backlog anger'. This is where anger builds up because we deny it or fail to deal with it. Avoid raking up old anger from the past. This will fuel the conflict rather than defuse or resolve it.

CONFRONTATION

Confront the situation using some of the techniques described in Skill 5 (see page 66).

RELEASE

Finally, let go of the destructive ways in which you abuse your anger, yourself and other people – for example, by punishing or blaming yourself and others. Allow yourself to forgive and to let go.

SKILL 7
PRIORITIZING YOUR TIME AND MANAGING YOURSELF

The ability to manage yourself and set priorities when undertaking projects is crucial. Many of us set off with good intentions, but leave too little time to complete what we need to do, become distracted or find that we are disorganized in our approach.

The main reference point for implementing our projects and change successfully is to have clear goals to work towards and to keep us focused (goal-setting is explored in detail in Section 3; see page 98). Skill 7 looks at how to ensure you work efficiently and smartly. In order to improve our use of time, it is important to understand where time goes. Our use of time can be categorized into two areas:

> **1 TIME SPENT ON USEFUL WORK   2 TIME WASTED**

Time spent on useful work needs to be maximized, while time wasted needs to be cut to a minimum. Five strategies for making the most efficient use of your time are highlighted below.

1 THE IMPORTANCE OF PLANNING

Managing time more effectively means planning time – both yours and others. Almost any task (writing, using the telephone, decorating a room, going on holiday) will be executed more effectively if a little time is given to planning it in advance. A sound plan of action, and the effective implementation of that plan, is the bridge across which an idea travels from the brain to the end result. Planning also allows you to handle several things within a project or change, and ensures that you give proper attention to each.

2 GOOD PLANNING

Once you have set your overall goals or objectives for your project or change, one of the most vital ingredients of planning is breaking a whole job down into parts and deciding the relative importance of each. Follow these five simple rules:

1 Gain firm **knowledge** of your project/change.
2 Leave a **margin for error** – don't plan over-tight deadlines.
3 Know your **resources** – human and material.
4 Plan **flexibility** so that you can make minor amendments where necessary.
5 Plan with **care**. Be pro-active rather than reactive.

Scheduling

To consolidate your time, schedule sensible blocks into your plan according to the nature of the task. For example, longer blocks will be necessary for writing the first draft of a book, and fewer, shorter ones for redrafting or amending the text. If feasible, try scheduling certain tasks on particular days of the week, and set aside parts of other days for working on major tasks.

Alternatively, schedule different activities into the day according to your own best working pattern. It makes sense to work on the most important part of your project when your energy levels are at their highest, namely your 'prime time'.

Know how long you can concentrate on one thing at any one time – this varies from individual to individual. Remember that working with other people demands longer blocks of time.

Plan your time carefully

3 USING A DIARY

A diary is an invaluable tool when planning any project or change, whether large or small. Adopting the following procedure will both help you in the planning stages and act as a reminder as the weeks and months progress.

PLAN YOUR YEAR

Write all the following items in your diary at the beginning of the year:

- **Known one-off events**

- **Holidays**

- **Family occasions**

- **Priority tasks or projects**

PLAN YOUR MONTH

At the start of each month, plan your diary as follows.

- **Take stock of unplanned days and identify what you want to use them for.**

- **Don't cancel days allocated to your priority tasks or projects.**

- **Make a point of attending important events.**

- **Reserve time for short-term important tasks.**

PLAN YOUR WEEK

Adopt effective weekly planning habits.

- **Have clear tasks/objectives for the week.**

- **Schedule in time for activities.**

PLAN YOUR DAY

Adopt effective daily time-management habits.

- **Create a daily plan first thing in the morning before you do anything else.**

- **Plan to do the hardest and most important things first.**

- **Review your daily objectives/tasks for five minutes at the end of the day and readjust your plan for the next day if necessary.**

Following the planning steps outlined above can make a significant difference to the effectiveness of your project-management skills. It has been proven over and over again that 1 hour of planning saves much more time in execution.

4 EFFECTIVE TIME MANAGEMENT

Having planned your project or change, it is important to manage your time effectively on a day-to-day basis. One way to approach this is to **eliminate** unnecessary tasks, **insulate** your schedule to allow you to use your blocked-out time for your projects and build in sufficient factors to your project to allow you time to **concentrate**.

Elimination

This involves, among other things, making sure you are not blindly following existing habits and practices. Eliminating could include:

- **Simplifying work practices** – for example, do you need a specialist to undertake specific parts of your project (such as Jane, see page 9, in her desire to employ a carpenter to build the wardrobes in her newly designed room)?
- **Better communication** – assertiveness can, as we have seen, defuse or avert conflicts and ensure that you make it clear to others what you want.
- **Delegating to others** – you don't have to do it on your own; who else can help you to free up your time so that you can undertake your projects?
- **Avoiding procrastination**, through developing courage and willpower.

Insulation

Think of your time in two parts: uncontrollable and controllable. **Uncontrollable time** includes things such as responding to others' demands and requests, phone calls, meetings and visitors. **Controllable time** is self-imposed and discretionary, and can be spent however you like.

Insulation means giving yourself an uninterrupted block of controllable time so that you can really utilize it effectively. Ideally, the block of time should coincide with your own 'prime' time, when your mental faculties are at their peak. It is then a good idea to group the uncontrollable time into similar task areas and put them together into specific time slots within the day. For example, setting aside half an hour at the beginning and end of the day to read and respond to e-mails. Make your plan very clear and have a 'quiet time' which is known to others, thereby increasing their co-operation.

Concentration

Concentrating means undertaking your important activities during your controllable time. Then you will be working most productively and avoiding spending too much of your time on unimportant tasks.

- It is often helpful to use lists as an aid to remind you what needs to be done. Tick off the items on your list as you achieve them, in order to keep you motivated. Be realistic about the size of your list. Only draw up achievable lists, or they can have a de-motivating effect when you fail to meet your daily objectives and tasks.
- Break down complex tasks into 'do-able' steps. Tackle each step, then a break. Don't try to concentrate for too long at a time.
- Be realistic – schedule only 50 per cent of your time, as the rest will undoubtedly be needed for uncontrollable events.
- Prioritize your tasks on a day-to-day basis, using your project goals and objectives as a guideline. Divide all your tasks into the following categories and undertake them in priority order.

PRIORITY 1	*Important and urgent (tasks to be undertaken immediately).*
PRIORITY 2	*Important but not urgent (tasks that can be planned in at a future time).*
PRIORITY 3	*Urgent but not important (tasks that can be allocated to someone else or delegated).*
PRIORITY 4	*Routine (tasks that need to be undertaken at some time but can be deferred or delegated).*

5 TOP TIME-SAVING TIPS

Outlined below are some time-saving tips to help you manage your projects and changes well. Identify those you already practise and a couple of others you would like to try out.

DOING LESS

Don't take work home from the office

Don't take on other people's problems where they should handle them themselves

Don't attend to issues other people can do better

Say no

Don't get bogged down in detail

Delegate

Discourage unnecessary meetings

WORKING FASTER/CUTTING DOWN TIME

Start and end meetings on time

When dealing with someone you think may waste time on a decision or implementation, set a target date (or, better still, get them to set one)

Use the telephone where it can save time

Tackle a task the first time the opportunity arises – don't put it off

Keep communications concise

Tackle important matters when you are more alert – it saves time and you make a wiser choice of options

Make deadlines and stick to them. Note them on a calendar

WORKING MORE EFFECTIVELY

Establish clearly your objectives

Make 'to be done' sheets daily, weekly

Use your diary more fully – plan the day and set times

Be realistic

Tackle jobs within your attention span

Take breaks during the day – a rest period revives you

Set priorities

Keep a neat work area

Plan all written communication

Schedule sensible time blocks

Build 'thinking time' into your day

Stick to agendas

Plan long phone calls

Each day, finish what you start

Be patient

Allow enough time for what you are doing – rushing can cause more work in the long run

Plan meetings

Plan your work and work your plan

Don't assume that everything that was important yesterday is important today

Work on the most important part of your project when your energy levels are at their highest

SKILL 8
EFFECTIVE DELEGATION

Most people know the basic principle of delegation, but the failure to convert this knowledge into practice can result in the busy person becoming over-loaded. Knowing what to delegate, and to whom, when making changes and implementing projects can reduce your stress levels and ensure that you maximize the use of your controllable time.

Peter: design report ✓
John: research ✓
Gail: calculate figures ✓
Chris: book meetings ✓

PRINCIPLES OF DELEGATION

The same principles apply at work or at home. The aim of delegation is to get others to do the work and make the decisions that they can handle as well as, or better than, you can. You can't do it all – you are only one person and no matter how skilled and energetic you are, there are limits to what you can accomplish. When you delegate, you become – in effect – many people, and you enlarge the scope of your achievement.

Delegation concerns deciding which tasks and responsibilities to retain and which to give to others. It therefore involves the following:

Planning – thinking about to whom you want to delegate, what you can delegate in its entirety and what others can help you with.

Decision-making – consciously deciding which responsibilities you want to keep for yourself and which you can share with others.

Organization – drawing up a plan of action and schedule for the task.

Co-ordination – making sure that you keep an overview of the tasks you have delegated and ensuring that deadlines are met.

Reviewing – checking on progress, adjusting deadlines and re-allcating tasks where necessary.

It is important to establish the limits of authority. When you delegate a task, also delegate the responsibility for doing it properly and the authority for getting it done. The other person should understand the importance of the task, the span of time they have to complete it and the degree of authority. For example, can they make a final decision? Agree with the person what sort of follow-up or review is necessary, and exactly what to expect. This is particularly important when the delegation is also a training or development exercise. You therefore need to:

Define aims – set objectives for the task.
Set standards – make clear the level of performance you require and set standards and boundaries around the task.
Coach the person to whom you have delegated the task – they may not get it right first time and will almost certainly need your support at some stage during the delegation process.
Establish deadlines – make these realistic and achievable, flexible where possible and co-ordinated with other tasks within the project.
Measure progress – set up regular review meetings or discussions and keep a note of important milestones.

WHAT SHOULD BE DELEGATED?

- Minor routine matters or matters that are urgent but not important.
- Tasks that assist in testing people's abilities, as well as giving them experience.
- Tasks where the person is able to do as well as, or better than, the person delegating the task.
- Jobs requiring the specialized skills of another person, for example Tony, the carpenter in Jane's decorating project (see page 54).

WHAT SHOULD *NOT* BE DELEGATED?

- All the work a person has to do.
- Emergency tasks requiring your own skill, knowledge and experience.
- Jobs requiring unofficial action.
- Matters that are an exception to policy or routine.
- Matters that might have serious repercussions.
- Work that is aimed at punishing or rewarding people.

The model outlined below can help you further with selecting what to delegate and to whom.

**WHAT AM I
GOING TO DELEGATE?**

**SKILLS
REQUIRED**

TASK

**TO WHOM SHOULD
I DELEGATE?**

TIME-SCALE

*You can't do it all
– you are only one person*

FAILING TO DELEGATE

We all have different reasons for not wanting to delegate. However, there is always room to delegate some responsibilities to another person. Here are some common reasons for failure to delegate.

Feeling indispensable – 'If I don't do it, no one else can or will'

Fear of loss of authority and need for control

Lack of confidence in others

Misguided benevolence and fear of over-loading the other person

Fear of being accused of 'dumping' unwanted tasks on others

Lacking delegation skills   **'I enjoy doing it myself'**

If you can get over the barrier of asking others for help, particularly when you are over-loaded or know that others have as much or more expertise, delegation can reap huge rewards.

GUIDELINES FOR DELEGATION

Follow these guidelines to ensure that you delegate well.

Build in regular reviews

Agree a schedule for the task

Tolerate mistakes – they are inevitable

Celebrate the successful completion of tasks

Ensure that the person concerned understands the extent of the delegation – set clear terms of reference, including levels of responsibility and authority

Praise and encourage the person to whom you have delegated the task

SKILL 9
HANDLING STRESS

Stress is our body's way of letting us know that the demands that are being placed upon us exceed our ability to cope. We all need a certain level of stress to survive as human beings. The physiological changes that take place in our body when it prepares to deal with a stressful situation, such as making a presentation in public or attending an interview, equip us to deal well and competently in these situations. Then, when the stressful situation passes, we return to a 'normal' state.

Problems arise, however, when we experience stress over an extended period of time, and our bodies are maintained at an unacceptable level of readiness. This state of being can, in both the short and longer term, create 'negative' symptoms that we need to watch out for and deal with.

Making changes and embarking upon projects can be stressful. It is useful to get to know our stress and how to deal with it if we are to be successful in implementing change that we want to introduce in our lives and work.

SYMPTOMS OF STRESS

These vary from individual to individual, but they can be divided into four main categories:

1 Physical symptoms – including palpitations, nausea, muscle cramps, aches and pains, colds and other infections, tiredness and indigestion.

2 Emotional symptoms – including mood swings, irritability, feeling tense, anxiety, withdrawal and feelings of powerlessness.

3 Behavioural symptoms – including accident-proneness, poor performance, over-eating or loss of appetite, lack of concentration, negativity, feeling drained.

4 Mental symptoms – including indecision, memory failure, worrying, muddled thinking, loss of sensitivity towards others, short-term thinking, loss of perspective.

To manage stress effectively get to know it in all its forms and learn to recognize when you are experiencing stress at an early stage.

CAUSES OF STRESS

Stress comes from four sources, known as 'stressors'.

1 Situational stressors come from our situation, our environment and our contemporary culture. They include unknown and unexpected situations, change, noise, depressing media reporting, poor housing, being confined in a vehicle and heavy workload.

2 Major life events that have a significant impact on our lives and our emotions. They include marriage, divorce, bereavement, birth of a child, moving house, ill health and financial worries.

3 Stressors caused by other people can be hard to handle. They include unreasonable demands or expectations, a bad atmosphere at work or at home and feeling that we are not understood.

4 Stressors from within ourselves can be the biggest cause of stress. They include seeking perfection, expectations of self, the need for purpose and success, feelings of inadequacy, the need to be in control and the need to be accepted and loved.

Learning more about the factors that cause you stress is a useful way of anticipating when you are likely to experience it. A single stressor is unlikely to create problems. Usually you experience a series of stressful events within a short period, and it is the cumulative effect of these events that causes the stress symptoms to emerge.

DEALING ASSERTIVELY WITH STRESS

Learning to handle stress in an assertive way can be an invaluable tool in interrupting the stress pattern and reducing your stress levels to manageable proportions. Stress can be debilitating if you allow it to continue without acknowledging and dealing with it. However, with a little practice, you can get to know your stress and welcome it as a life-saving tool. The following strategies should be helpful.

Become knowledgeable about stress

Ask yourself the following questions in relation to a stressful situation that you have experienced or are currently experiencing, or that has become a repeating pattern.

'What causes this stress?'

'What can I do to reduce my level of stress in this situation?'

'Why do I react this way?'

'Do I affect anyone else?'

'When and where does it happen?'

'Who can I ask to support me?'

'How does it affect me?'

Come to terms with your feelings

Acknowledge your feelings and share them with others. Emotions are a valuable indicator that things are either going well or not. Try not to deny your feelings but rather accept them as valuable friends.

Develop effective behavioural skills

Ask for your needs to be met, avoid blaming others, use your free time productively, learn to say no and yes, acknowledge problems as soon as they appear, take the initiative and develop your sense of personal power.

Establish and maintain a strong support network

Don't be afraid to ask for direct help, rid yourself of destructive or non-supportive relationships and tell the members of your support network that you value their friendship.

Develop a lifestyle to strengthen you against stress

Build in a little exercise each day, find time for relaxation, plan your use of time both in the long and short term, eat a healthy diet, do not use tobacco and avoid the consumption of alcohol and caffeine, except in moderate amounts.

Look after your mental health

Think positively, handle your negative inner voice, know your limits, do things you enjoy and spend time on hobbies and special projects.

HOW DO YOU HANDLE STRESS?

Answer the following questions to check how you handle stress right now.

1 *What factors are present in your life and work at the moment that are causing you stress?*

2 *How do these stressors affect you:*
- physically?
- emotionally?
- mentally?
- behaviourally?

3 *Do you typically respond to stress by:*
- acknowledging and dealing with it?
- denying it?
- ignoring it?

4 *What might you do to manage your stress levels better in the future?*

TURNING STRESS TO YOUR ADVANTAGE

You can use stress positively by keeping it within manageable levels, and channelling the stress that fuels your energy sources into the projects and changes that you want to make. One of the key things that you can do to achieve this during your projects and changes is to focus on those areas over which you have control.

During projects many of us spend a lot of time worrying about things over which we have no, or little, control. We waste a lot of time and energy in doing this. We can also waste time by failing to take action in relation to certain aspects of our projects that we can control, and instead procrastinate.

Both of these strategies cause us to experience frustration and stress from within ourselves. The diagram below illustrates this:

	CAN CONTROL	**CAN'T CONTROL**
TAKE ACTION	ACHIEVEMENT	CONTINUOUS STRIVING
TAKE NO ACTION	GIVING UP	LETTING GO

Learn to recognize when you are experiencing stress

Case study

Nigel spent quite a lot of time worrying about the decline of the returns on his investments, and his levels of stress increased each time he read a newspaper or heard a financial report on the television news. Eventually, he realized that he was worrying over something over which he had no control; he could not influence how the financial markets performed. His continuous striving was wasting energy and increasing his anxiety and fear. It was threatening to sabotage his goal.

So he decided to separate out the aspect of his finances over which he had control, namely how he responded to the economic downturn. By focusing on the area over which he had control, he was able to take action by seeking professional advice and adjusting his plan accordingly.

His anxiety levels dropped immediately, because he had taken action over something he could control and let go of worrying about things over which he had no control.

TAKING CONTROL

Try this out for yourself. Think of a situation that currently causes you stress and answer the following questions:

- Which of those factors that cause you stress have you little or no control over?
- Which factors do you have control over?
- How could you let go of worrying about those factors over which you have no or little control?
- What steps might you take to deal with those factors over which you have control?

By dealing with situations in this way, you can take control and move things forward, without worrying unnecessarily. Ask a friend for help if you need to – remember you don't have to do this all on your own.

SKILL 10
MAINTAINING HIGH SELF-ESTEEM

In order to achieve success in getting our projects started and being able to see them through to the end, we need to be able to handle the knocks, setbacks and rejections that will inevitably occur. This is not always easy, as it means keeping our self-esteem at a consistently high level so that we can develop resilience and maintain the belief that we will succeed despite the barriers that might present themselves. Self-esteem is essential to our well-being and it is something that can be grown, or allowed to diminish.

WHAT IS SELF-ESTEEM?

Although 'self-esteem' has been discussed already in this book, it might be useful to spend a little more time defining the term, and identifying strategies to maintain it at a high level. Self-esteem can be divided into two types.

First type

Internal sense of self-worth This is the ability to like and accept yourself with all your strengths and weaknesses. Having high internal self-esteem is not about being perfect; it is about accepting yourself as equal to others, while recognizing that you are different and unique. It also includes accepting others in the same way, rather than as superior or inferior to you.

Second type

External sense of self-worth This is the type of self-esteem that is reflected by other people. We get it from the positive or negative comments of others and the need for their approval and acceptance. They do this in all sorts of ways, such as wanting to spend time with us, giving us praise or seeking our advice. Other external sources of our self-esteem are the media, work and relationships.

Most people rely heavily on external sources of self-esteem. This is a risky strategy, since it means that we might not get what we want from others, or conflicting messages cause it to be inconsistent, resulting in our self-esteem going up and down from day to day. For example, we might receive praise from our boss for working long hours on a project to get it finished and at the same time be criticized by our partner for never being at home.

DEVELOPING INTERNAL SELF-ESTEEM

The secret of maintaining high self-esteem is to develop the sources of internal self-esteem that will build a solid foundation that is difficult to knock down. Then, when the inevitable knocks and setbacks arise during our projects, we can quickly bounce back without our self-esteem being diminished. It is like comparing self-esteem to a tree:

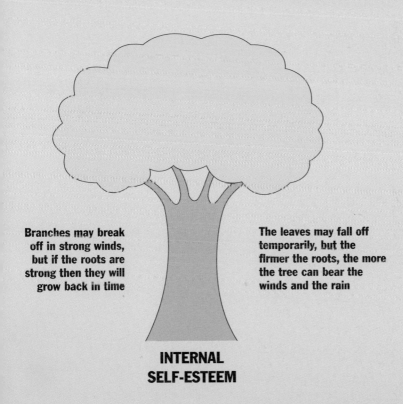

Branches may break off in strong winds, but if the roots are strong then they will grow back in time

The leaves may fall off temporarily, but the firmer the roots, the more the tree can bear the winds and the rain

INTERNAL SELF-ESTEEM

The key skills and strategies that you need to adopt when undertaking projects are all covered in this book. Applying these skills and strategies will assist you in successfully developing your internal sources of self-esteem.

Building self-esteem in the long term can be achieved by:

challenging your negative inner voice

taking the initiative

practising assertive behaviour

setting goals

developing motivation and willpower

being aware of your self-growth and development

taking physical and emotional care of yourself

putting yourself first

giving quality time to yourself

taking risks

In addition, ask yourself the following questions:

How much of what I do is based on a need for reflected approval?

Whose eyes reflect back my measure of acceptability?

What standards do I have to measure up to?

Whose standards do I need to reach in order to qualify for acceptance within each category of my life – at work, at home, in relationships with others?

It is only by developing self-acceptance that we can build up our self-esteem. To do this, ask yourself these questions:

With those people, is there a conflict between what I do to please them and what I really want to do?

Whose opinion does matter to me?

Remember that it is all right if we are making a choice to please these other people.

Self-esteem is essential to our well-being

Section 3 continues to build on the skills described in Section 2, but focuses on the mechanics of identifying projects, setting and reviewing goals, and monitoring and celebrating success.

Section 3

10 stages to success

Section 1 helped you identify your **strengths** and **weaknesses**. **Section 2** outlined some of the **skills** and **strategies** you will need to develop to ensure success with your projects and changes.

This section follows a structured route to satisfactorily starting up and completing projects, from identifying priorities for change to implementation and review. You should use your Personal Journal to make notes where appropriate.

STAGE 1
IDENTIFYING AREAS OF DISSATISFACTION

The Introduction presented the change equation (see page 8) and identified how you can use the equation to help you know when you are ready for change. It can be helpful to think of the different aspects of your life and work, and to use the equation to identify the areas or relationships that you are currently dissatisfied with.

Having identified your key areas of dissatisfaction, and because people often want to make several changes in their lives and work at the same time, Stage 1 examines a method to help you identify your priorities for change. This will also assist you to set in place some desired outcomes or vision for the changes and projects that you want to make. The method is called **domain mapping**.

DRAWING UP A DOMAIN MAP

A domain map consists of a series of concentric circles, broken up into segments, with you at the centre. Each segment constitutes a 'domain'. Imagine you are standing on the summit of a mountain, looking down on the domains which represent the areas in your life that are causing you concern and with which you have some form of relationship (this can be a person or an aspect of your life). The domain map is completed in several stages.

STAGE 1

STAGE 2

STAGE 3

Stage 1 In the first circle away from the centre, write in each segment an area of your life that you are dissatisfied with.

Stage 2 Then write in the corresponding segment of the next circle, for each domain, a description of the present situation.

Stage 3 Then go out to the next circle and describe how you would like that situation to be.

Case study

In the Introduction (see page 7), Pat was considering a career change because she had come to a point where she would not be able to use all of the skills she had acquired within her organization. Pat's situation at that time is helpful when illustrating how to draw up a domain map. At Stage 1, Pat allocated one segment to her career. In addition, however, there were other areas in Pat's life that she was dissatisfied with.

- She had no balance in her life. It consisted of all work and no play, she had no time for herself and her exercise routine had dropped off.
- She had a difficult relationship with her brother that she wanted to improve.
- She wanted to create more space in her house by building an extension.
- She found it difficult to be assertive at work with certain key people and in certain situations.

Each of these areas was represented within a separate segment or domain. You can see from the diagram how Pat completed the first three stages of her domain map, using the 'assertive behaviour at work' domain as an example. This gave her a 'bird's-eye view' of the aspects of her life that she was currently dissatisfied with, and also some idea of how she wanted things to be, following any changes she made.

STAGE 2
IDENTIFYING PRIORITIES FOR CHANGE

In determining your priorities for change, you will need to identify which of the desired outcomes, set out in the third circle of the domain map, you want to begin working on first. How you choose your priorities will depend on your own sense of what your priorities might be.

MAKING DECISIONS

Here are some possible criteria to help you to decide.

Importance – it is the most important because it will bring about the biggest pay-off for yourself and others.

Urgency – the effects of not tackling it will be the most serious.

Quickest benefit – it will show some results very soon.

Hardest to deal with – it is the most difficult, so you want to do it first to get it completed and out of the way.

Key to some of the other domains – it needs to be undertaken first because until this change is made, you can't move forward on the others.

Will – how much do you really want things to change?

Set your priorities and make things change

Case study

Pat set her priorities for change in the following order.

PRIORITY 1	**Become more assertive with key people at work** *Necessary in negotiating a career move and to help her to determine exactly what she wanted. Pat felt that she would see beneficial results in a short space of time.*
PRIORITY 2	**Make a career change** *A key area as it affected other changes. She had a huge amount of will to make this change.*
PRIORITY 3	**Build in time for herself** *An important priority because Pat would need time to plan her career change. She would also have to look after her physical and emotional well-being in making such a big career change.*
PRIORITY 4	**Establish a better relationship with her brother** *Although it was important to do this at some time, there were other more urgent priorities.*
PRIORITY 5	**Make a change in her living accommodation** *Pat decided that she did not want to risk the financial outlay at this stage. In addition, if she was to become self-employed, Pat might need to rethink her living space to fit in a home office.*

Priority 1 became Pat's immediate focus of attention because it equipped her with one of the key skills required to get her second priority started (see page 50). The project Pat identified was relatively easy. She identified the support she needed, then practised her new skills in influencing the HR Director. An assertiveness course helped her to develop her skills further.

STAGE 3
SETTING GOALS AND ACHIEVING THEM

Only 4–5 per cent of people set goals, and yet over 90 per cent of those who do set goals achieve them. Setting goals is an excellent way to raise the probability of success in implementing your projects and changes.

So why do so few people set goals? Some of the reasons were explored in Section 1 (see page 14). Remember there are those of us who prefer to plan for tomorrow and those who prefer to live for today. Other reasons for not setting goals are:

We don't know how to – we lack a method or formula for setting goals.
We don't have the time – we don't set aside time because we are too busy.
Fear of failure – if we don't have goals, we won't fail.
We can't see the point – 'How will goals help me to achieve what I want to?'
We don't see the need – 'They're unnecessary, I'll just get on with it.'

This stage shows you how to set goals with the minimum of effort and the maximum probability of success.

TRADITIONAL GOAL-SETTING

The traditional way of setting goals is to use a formula that is very precise and produces goals that are:
Specific, **M**easurable, **A**ctionable, **R**ealistic, **T**ime orientated.

SMART objectives are very effective when used within organizations and business environments where goals need to be measured precisely and achieved within a set time-frame; for example, the goals that are set within staff appraisals. There is, however, an alternative approach, which is more flexible and more suitable for the types of projects and changes that you will be embarking upon.

AN ALTERNATIVE APPROACH

This approach requires you to trust in the goal-setting process and to assume that you will succeed. It also requires you to think big and to expect the best. Here are some guidelines:

Set your goals as large as possible – think big. This will create excitement, the desire to achieve your goals and a sense of challenge.

Be specific in describing your goals – a clear statement can be helpful in keeping you focused. Writing your goals in the present tense as if you have already achieved them can be a very powerful tool. This helps to create the belief that you can achieve your goals.

Write your goals down and tell others about them. They can be written down in the literal sense, but it is also a good idea to include pictures, objects and other representational items to describe them.

Use both logic and creativity in developing your goals – for example, use visualization exercises to help you.

List the blocks and barriers between you and your goals, and formulate a plan to overcome them.

Break down the tasks involved into daily units.

Discipline yourself to take the necessary steps to achieve your goals – develop your willpower.

Don't worry too much about how to achieve your goals – having some clear first steps worked out is often a more effective approach than a detailed plan of action.

Be flexible, review your goals from time to time and adjust them where necessary – for example, if you need more time.

Assume success rather than failure, and try not to concern yourself about whether you can or cannot achieve your goals. Learn to trust that the process will deliver them. This creates an expectation that the goals will be achieved.

Take responsibility for the outcome.

Reward yourself when you achieve your goals.

Case study

Future mapping

Nigel was planning a move to another part of the country for his retirement (see page 7). He set the following goal and wrote it in the present tense as if he had already achieved it. This process is called 'future mapping'.

It is July 2004 and I am now living in a new property in the countryside with my partner Elise and our dog Barney. The house has been built to my own specification and I have sufficient funds in the bank and a good pension to enable me to retire from my job in the city.

Nigel set his goal five years earlier; however, by writing it down as if he had already achieved it, he felt motivated and driven towards achieving his goal.

Achieving your goal

Nigel succeeded by implementing the 10 key guidelines detailed below.

1 Thinking big

Nigel was not originally going to build his own home, but he had been looking for a property for some time and had found nothing suitable. He therefore developed an ambitious plan to have a house built to his specification.

2 Writing it down

He wrote down his goal, but he also gathered together lots of pictures of the type of house he wanted and put these in a folder with pictures of his partner and their dog, together with pictures of the area.

3 Involving others

He involved his family and friends in his dream so that it became more real and enabled them to share in his goal.

4 Visualizing

He used visualization techniques to create in his mind a picture of the perfect house, and a sense of how the house would look once decorated.

5 Planning

Nigel developed annual, monthly, weekly and daily planning systems which broke his plan down into smaller tasks that did not daunt him. He avoided fine detail but set some key milestones and first steps to achieve.

6 Overcoming barriers

There were lots of barriers threatening to stop Nigel. There was the problem of the stock-market downturn which reduced his pension (see pages 7 and 87). He had to adjust his thinking about the type of house he wanted and made alterations to the size of the property to cut costs. He dealt with each barrier as it arose and developed strategies to remove them.

7 Reviewing

He also reviewed his goal regularly to check that he was still on course and to adjust time-scales. This was particularly important during the building of his property, when bad weather, shortage of labour etc., delayed completion.

8 Thinking positively

He developed positive thinking by repeating affirmations to himself on a regular basis and enlisting the support of his family and friends.

9 Focusing

Nigel also kept focused on his goal by making sure that other projects did not take him away from his first priority.

10 Succeeding

Nigel is due to move into his new property next year. There is some way to go but he has an expectation of success and is already planning the celebration party. So you can see from Nigel's example that it is possible to set goals and achieve them. The process need not be too demanding and, having the desire, belief and expectation that the goal will succeed, he will ensure that he becomes one of the 90 per cent of people who achieve their goals.

Section 4 will guide you through the goal-setting process to ensure that you give yourself the best chance of success.

STAGE 4
IDENTIFYING AND PLANNING FIRST STEPS

The primary function of the goal-setting process is to help you create a vision of how you want a particular situation to look like in the future. Rather than making a detailed action plan that sets out how to achieve your goal, as in the traditional method of goal-setting, developing one or two first steps towards your goal can be a more encouraging way of completing your projects. Seeing the achievement of your goal as a series of steps makes it a much more manageable process and easier to break down into bite-sized pieces.

THE FIRST STEPS

Imagine that you are a new manager. Your goal is to learn to manage staff effectively and to develop some basic management skills. The first step might be to identify the key management skills that you need to develop in order to fulfil your role as a first-time manager, and to analyse your strengths and weaknesses against these skills.

It can be quite easy to identify and plan a first step, but sometimes difficult to carry it out, so you may need help from others. For example, in the above situation, you may need to ask colleagues for their feedback to help you identify your strengths and weaknesses, or you might need to consult more experienced managers. You may need to draw on your Resource Pack of skills in Section 2, such as using assertiveness, to ask for feedback.

USING YOUR DOMAIN MAP

Return to your domain map and draw a fourth concentric circle around the outside. Record your first steps in the relevant sections.

STAGE 5
REVEIWING YOUR GOALS AND FIRST STEPS

When you have implemented your first step, it is important to review it.

THE LEARNING CYCLE

The review process has four stages:

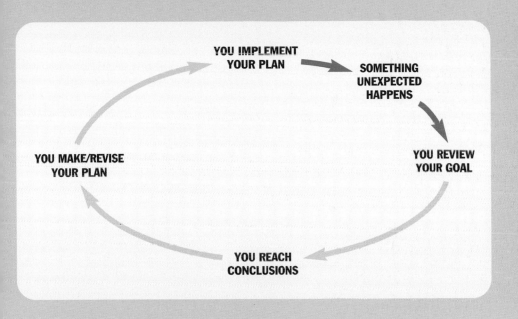

This model assumes that learning is a continuous process, and that, to learn effectively, we need to complete the cycle. You can use the model to review your first steps and goals when the unexpected happens, or when you have completed your first step. It can also be used for periodically reviewing your goals.

Case study

Reviewing your goals

At one stage during his project, Nigel planned to sell his house and buy a less expensive property as his city base. The intention was to rent the property out for most of the year, except between September and November, when he planned to return to the city each year.

1 Nigel sold his house and purchased another property as planned **(implementing his plan)**.

2 Then something unexpected happened. The stock-market decline reduced the value of his pension fund and he needed to thin again about the 'luxury' of retaining a property in the city **(reviewing his goal)**.

3 He sought expert advice from the bank and his financial adviser **(reaching conclusions)**.

4 He decided to sell the property and invest the profit to supplement his pension **(revising his plan)**.

By taking time out to review his goal in the light of an unexpected event, he was able to make a further decision in relation to his project that brought about an improvement in his financial stability.

REVIEWING YOUR FIRST STEPS

This involves going through a similar process of review. Taking the example of the new manager again (see page 102), when you have analysed your strengths and weaknesses, you will need to decide what you will do next to meet your development needs. You might opt to attend a management training course and, following your attendance on the course, undertake a review of how the course helped you to move towards your overall goal.

STEP 1

You review the course and identify what you have learned. You monitor your performance over a month and identify where you have improved your management skills and confidence and where you still need help.

STEP 2

You reach conclusions; perhaps you need more help in a particular area.

STEP 3

You plan your next step. How might you get further help? Do you need more formal training or would finding a mentor be a more appropriate course of action?

STEP 4

You implement the plan by taking the next step, with help where necessary.

Thus the process of review can help you evaluate and set further steps in place. Develop the self-discipline to review your first steps at regular intervals, and to review your goals when something happens that might affect them.

STAGE 6
EVALUATING OTHER COURSES OF ACTION

When you have identified and implemented your first step, you will often find that your next step involves examining different possibilities and courses of action. This will involve you weighing up the pros and cons for each of your possible choices and identifying your preferred option.

WEIGHING UP THE PROS AND CONS

Here is a method that will enable you to weigh up the pros and cons of each course of action. You simply draw the diagram opposite in your Personal Portfolio and complete it for each possible course of action. It is a simple process that is effective in that it helps you to be objective about making choices.

The example of the new manager and the different options available to them for addressing their development needs illustrates how you might use the method for your projects.

Don't neglect your feelings

Option 1 TRAINING COURSE	PROS: - Meet other people - Quick - Share good practice - Company will pay	CONS: - Terrified of looking stupid in a group - General – not specific	CONLUSION: Not now
Option 2 DISTANCE LEARNING	PROS: - Flexible - Do it in my own time/on my own - Easy to understand	CONS: - Boring - Not good for skills practice	CONLUSION: Only as a supplement to other methods
Option 3 MENTORING	PROS: - One to one - Job specific - Personally tailored - Confidential	CONS: - Only me and mentor - Not quite so good for learning skills	CONLUSION: Consider as an option

THINKING AND FEELING

Use your thinking ability to identify pros and cons, but don't neglect your feelings. In the example one way to meet the new manager's training and development needs would be to attend a training course. There might be a list of pros in favour of this course of action.

But what if you had a fear of being in a group? This would mean listening to your feelings and identifying your fear as a con, which you would need to overcome. Your feelings have, in this case, given you an insight into a possible barrier to achieving one of your options.

By analysing your pros and cons at a thinking and feeling level, you can gain a better insight into what choices to make.

STAGE 7
REMOVING BARRIERS TO SUCCESS

One of the main things that can hinder us from achieving our goals and completing our projects is failing to identify and remove the barriers that appear from time to time.

SELECTING OPTIONS

In the example of the new manager, one of the cons that was identified for the management training course option was a fear of being with a group of people. One way of dealing with this con would be to select another option, such as reading a management textbook. However, apart from this particular con, the training course would have been one of your preferred options.

An alternative course of action, therefore, would be to deal with your fear of being in a group, by using some of the skills from your Resource Pack (see Section 2), such as challenging your negative inner voice, or using some of the initiating strategies in the assertiveness skill (see page 46).

FORCE-FIELD ANALYSIS

When you are making changes, for every positive step you take towards the change, an equal and opposite negative force will meet it. To progress, it is essential to move the negative forces out of the way. This can be achieved through a method called force-field analysis, where the positive and negative forces are examined and strategies are developed in order to remove the negative forces and build on the positive ones. The process of force-field analysis can be used at the beginning of a project, when setting your goals, as well as during the project when you encounter difficulties.

Case study

Pat was thinking of a career change (see page 7). At the beginning of her project, she analysed the positive and negative forces that existed in relation to her goal, which she set in the present, as if she had already achieved it. Similarly, Pat used the force-field analysis technique as if she was looking back in time, imagining that she had identified and removed the barriers that existed in relation to her goal. By writing them down as if she had already succeeded in removing them, she felt more confident and motivated to develop strategies to deal with them in the present. Her method is set out below.

Pat's goal was: 'It is 2004 and I am working as a freelance management development consultant with a variety of clients who provide me with regular work.' First, Pat identified all the positive and negative forces that were present in relation to her goal. Some of these are highlighted on the diagram below:

POSITIVE FORCES

| Skills level good | Motivation good | Have good networks | Can work for clients in free time | Backing of HR |

| Lose team spirit | Financial management poor | Lose security of current job | Fear of failure | Work/life balance will suffer (short term) |

NEGATIVE FORCES

The next thing that Pat did was to make a list of steps to remove or get round the barriers, using as a resource some of the positive forces and the skills from her Resource Pack (see Section 2), and looking back as if she had already achieved the steps.

'To remove the barriers facing me, I have:

'**built up my network of fellow freelance consultants and arranged to meet them at regular intervals.**'

'**attended a financial management seminar and found a good accountant and financial adviser.**'

'**negotiated a clause in my severance package so that I can return to my previous organization within two years.**'

'**assumed I would succeed and found myself a mentor to help me think through difficult situations and to provide me with support.**'

'**given myself three years to build my new business, and developed the willpower to block out time for me, and the family, in my diary at the beginning of each year.**'

By writing down the list of steps, Pat developed a mini action plan, and, because in her mind she had already completed it, she found it relatively easy to implement.

Plan of action

1

2

3

4

MAKING THINGS HAPPEN

If you don't remove the barriers to success, they will get in the way of your changes and result in you feeling defeated or lacking in motivation. In developing your strategies to remove your barriers, it is important to put your energy into things over which you have control and delegate or forget about the things over which you have no or little control. Then you will be able to make things happen, without further barriers getting in your way.

For example, if Pat had tried to undertake all of the financial management side of her new business without the support of expert help, she would have been setting herself a task that was over-ambitious and not fully within her control. She lacked the specialist accountancy and financial advice skills that she needed others to undertake on her behalf, to ensure that the financial management of her business flowed smoothly. She therefore did the minimum that was necessary to introduce herself to the things she needed to know about financial matters, and delegated the rest.

Notice how Pat also drew on her skills Resource Pack in developing and implementing the key steps to remove the barriers that were in danger of sabotaging her goal.

To progress, move negative forces out of the way

STAGE 8
KNOWING WHEN YOU HAVE REACHED YOUR GOAL

It is important that you have ways of measuring when you have completed your projects and achieved your goals. Many experts recommend that, with any project, you should identify some key 'success criteria' that can be measured and can provide an indicator that the project has been completed or the goal has been reached.

DEVELOPING SUCCESS CRITERIA

There are several ways of developing success criteria. The first method below uses the technique of visualization to evaluate whether or not you have reached your goals, but there is also an alternative for those who are uncomfortable with visualization.

Visualization exercise

This will help you visualize what your project or goal will look like when you have achieved it using your creativity to develop a clear picture of success.

1   Start by doing a short relaxation exercise (see page 136).
2   Keep your eyes closed and imagine that you have achieved your goal. Begin to create a clear mental picture of:
    What it feels like (do you feel excited, elated, empowered, happy and so on?).
    What it looks like (what pictures do you see in your mind?).
    Whether there are any sounds you associate with it (what can you hear?).
    Whether there are any tactile elements present (what can you touch?).
3   Stay relaxed until you develop a clear sensory picture of your goal.
4   When you open your eyes, make a note in your Personal Portfolio of any images that you want to record. These will represent your success criteria.

AN ALTERNATIVE APPROACH

If you prefer to use a more tangible and logical method of developing success criteria, you will need to revisit your goal, written in the present tense. You can then ask yourself the following question: 'Now that I have achieved my goal, what are the key criteria that inform me that I have been successful in reaching my goal?'

Here are the answers for some of the examples given in this book.

Nigel would have some tangible success criteria, including a house in an area that he wants to live in, a lifestyle that enables him to dine out once a week and more choice to live the lifestyle he wants to following his retirement.

Pat would also have some tangibles, including a database of clients; an office; a network of associates.

Jane would have a redesigned room that meets her redefined needs.

Even with this method, however, it is useful to bring in some sensory data, such as:

How do **Pat** and **Nigel** feel when they have achieved success in implementing their changes?

What can **Jane** see, smell and touch when her decorating project is complete?

Whichever method you use, identifying success criteria is a very important part of getting things done.

STAGE 9
AVOIDING 'CHANGE-BACK' MESSAGES

Many of us, when we make changes, affect other people by the changes that we make. Not everybody likes these changes, particularly if they have not been involved in developing the project from the beginning.

Case study

Nigel had his retirement plan in place some years before he met Elise, his partner. It was important for him to involve Elise in his project as soon as they met, because the move would have a big impact on her life.

At first, Elise was unhappy about the proposed move. However, through Nigel involving her in his plans, using some of the skills in his Resource Pack, she gradually adopted his goal. Nigel was always prepared to compromise. If the area he wanted to move to did not suit Elise, he was happy to look at other options.

Nigel did not receive too many 'change-back' messages that would have diverted him from his lifelong goal, but this is not always the case.

STAYING ON COURSE

Imagine that you have always behaved in a passive way in dealing with your boss. One example of this is that you have always said yes to a request to work late. You then decide to make a change and begin to say no when asked to put in extra time. You do this in an assertive way, building in a compromise in that you agree to work late if the issue is important and urgent, but not as a general rule. Suddenly, your boss sees a change of behaviour, which may not meet his needs, and he might try various tactics to get you to 'change back'. You then have a couple of choices:

- **Change back to the way things were before.**
- **Stick with the change, since you know it is a reasonable thing to do and you feel perfectly within your rights.**

The second course of action takes courage, but if you stick with your resolve, the other person will eventually have to make a choice about whether to continue to put pressure on you to 'change back', or to accept the change and adapt their behaviour in line with your new approach. Research has shown that, very often, the other person will adapt if the change is reasonable and you stick with your resolve.

Strategies for avoiding the risk of 'changing back'

✓ Revisit your goal and remind yourself why you made the change.
✓ Weigh up the pros and cons of the two options – changing back and sticking to your resolve.
✓ Use your assertive skills to influence and persuade the other person.
✓ Involve the other person in your project so that they develop 'ownership'.
✓ Practise developing your willpower.
✓ Identify the benefits for the other person of the change you are making.

By sticking with your goals you are likely to achieving your overall aims. Remember, however, the change equation (see page 8). If the cost of any change is too high, then **adapt**, **postpone** or **reconsider** your goals.

STAGE 10
LEARNING FROM FAILURE AND CELEBRATING SUCCESS

Things rarely go perfectly, and you will experience both failure and success in achieving your goals. Both these extremes can be used to positive advantage.

SURVIVING AND LEARNING FROM FAILURE

In Stage 5, the learning cycle assisted you to review your first steps and goals. This model can also be used to identify the things that have gone less well and that you would consider to be failures. No one likes to fail, but when you ask people what they have learned from most in their lives, it is the failures that have taught them the valuable lessons that build up their wisdom and insights.

The process of review is important here. Use the method of reviewing success described in Section 1 (see page 14) and the learning cycle (see page 103) to assist you in reviewing your failures. Here are some things you can do to make failure less painful.

 Be pro-active. Use the learning review process to write down the key learning points, and promise yourself to change the way you do things. Ask yourself 'What will I do differently next time?' Make a note of your insights in your Personal Portfolio.

Celebrate it. Failure does not need to be the end of the world. Treat yourself to something you enjoy doing or allow yourself an indulgence.

Don't be embarrassed. Try to let go of the shame or humiliation you might feel as a result of failing – we all fail sometimes.

Share your feelings. Talk about your failure to a friend. This helps to get things off your chest and develop a sense of perspective.

Learn to laugh at yourself. Is there anything that you find even slightly funny or amusing about your failure?

Learn to forgive yourself. We all make mistakes and there is always another day.

CELEBRATING SUCCESS

Remember to reward yourself for your successes. Many of us complete one project and then move on to the next one, without taking time for breath. We can also fall into the trap of underplaying our success by putting it down to good luck, or by minimizing the skills and effort that we put into achieving our goals.

In the same way that we can use the learning review process to review our failures, we can also use it to review our successes. Review your projects following their completion and draw out the things that went well and not so well. Celebrating success includes:

- Acknowledging the skills that assisted you to achieve your goals.
- Recognizing the input and energy that brought about your success.
- Daring to boast a little about how skilful, talented and focused you have been in achieving your goals.
- Organizing a celebration to share with friends and family, so that they can also join in your success.
- Treating yourself to something special, just for you – putting yourself first.
- Accepting compliments from others who acknowledge and congratulate you on your success.

Many of us find the process of celebrating success difficult. Build it into your willpower exercises by giving yourself a treat when you have completed a difficult stage of your project. Make celebrating even your minor successes habit-forming.

Allowing yourself to handle your failures well and celebrate success will provide you with the learning, enthusiasm and motivation to achieve success in all that you undertake in the future. Don't miss out this extremely important part of the project process – you deserve it! Now turn to Section 4 to learn how to plan and implement your own projects.

Section 4
Practical exercises

This section guides you through some simple exercises in relation to your chosen project, in order to assist you with its implementation and to check your understanding of the concepts described in this book. Use your Personal Portfolio to make notes as you go through the exercises. Everything you need to know to ensure you succeed in the projects that you undertake has been covered.

Now is the time to take a leap and say to yourself **'Just do it!'**

EXERCISE 1
IDENTIFYING AREAS OF DISSATISFACTION AND CREATING A DOMAIN MAP

Use the change equation to identify your areas of dissatisfaction:

Change = dissatisfaction + vision + first steps > cost involved

Think of the different aspects of your life and make a note of the areas or relationships that you are currently dissatisfied with:

Dissatisfaction:

Dissatisfaction:

Dissatisfaction:

Dissatisfaction:

Compile a domain map representing your key areas of dissatisfaction. Draw a circle that represents you, and then draw the first three concentric circles of your domain map, highlighting:

- those areas of dissatisfaction where you want to make changes (first concentric circle);
- a description of the current situation (second concentric circle), i.e. what it is like right now;
- your vision for the future, i.e. writing a statement of how you would like the situation to be (third concentric circle).

EXERCISE 2
IDENTIFYING PRIORITIES FOR CHANGE

TURN YOUR VISION INTO A CHALLENGE

This exercise helps you to translate what you would like to achieve from the statement of your vision in the third circle of your domain map into an action-orientated statement.

Turn your dreams and visions into challenges by rephrasing them:

I will...

I will...

I will ..

I will...

ASSESS YOUR WILL TO CHANGE

Make sure that you have the will to undertake your challenges. How much do you really want to change the areas of your life and work with which you are dissatisfied? Take each challenge one by one and ask yourself these questions:

? What are the pay-offs, or short-term gains, for me if I stay with things as they are right now?

? What are the long-term negative consequences if I don't make the changes I want to make?

? What will be the benefits of change?

? Are there any negative effects of change that I will need to manage when change happens?

PRIORITIZE YOUR CHALLENGES
TO SELECT YOUR FIRST PROJECT

Use these prioritizing criteria to help you to select your first project:

- How important is it – will there be serious consequences if I don't do it soon?
- Will it show some results very soon – is this a motivational quick-fix project?
- Is it the hardest project to deal with – do I want to do it first and get my most difficult challenge out of the way?
- Is it key to some of the other domains – does it need to be undertaken first because, until this change is made, I can't move forward on the others?
- How much do I really want to make this happen?

EXERCISE 3
SETTING GOALS

Translate your challenge into a clear goal using the future mapping exercise in Section 3 (see page 100). Remember to write your goal down as if you have already achieved it.

There may be more than one goal, or your goal may be broken down into several subsidiary goals. Develop a separate goal statement for each goal and each subgoal. Remember to include a date in your goal statement so that you have a time-scale to work towards.

It is [date] and I am...

It is [date] and I am...

It is [date] and I am...

It is [date] and I am...

Gather any other material that you want to keep with your goals, such as pictures or photographs. Tell people about your goals and begin to involve the key people who will be affected by your goals.

EXERCISE 4
IDENTIFYING SUCCESS CRITERIA

Use either of the methods described in Section 3 (see page 112) to identify your key success criteria. These will provide you with a way of measuring when you have achieved your goals.

My key success criteria are:

1

2

3

4

EXERCISE 5
REMOVING BARRIERS TO SUCCESS

Using the force-field analysis described in Section 3 (see page 108), write down your goal and identify all the positive and negative forces that exist in relation to it. Plot them on a diagram, like the one below, in your Personal Portfolio.

My goal is:

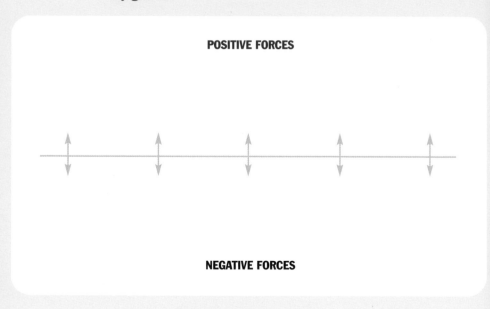

POSITIVE FORCES

NEGATIVE FORCES

Next, keeping your thinking in the past, write down all the things that you have done to build on the positive forces and remove the negative ones.

To remove the barriers that faced me in achieving my goal, I have:

1
2
3
4
5

EXERCISE 6
IDENTIFYING KEY STAKEHOLDERS

Undertake a stakeholder analysis (see page 52) for the project or change that you are tackling. Make sure that you don't forget anyone, and select one or two key people whom you think it will be particularly important to influence within your project. It is also useful, at this stage of the project, to identify the people who will assist you or to whom you might delegate.

My key stakeholders are:

1
2
3
4
5

The people whom it will be most important to influence if I am going to succeed with this project are:

1
2
3
4
5

The people that I will need help from on the project are:

1
2
3
4
5

The people to whom I could delegate some of my tasks during the project are:

1
2
3
4
5

EXERCISE 7
IDENTIFYING FIRST STEPS

Remember that seeing the achievement of your goal as a series of steps makes it a much more manageable process and easier to break down into bite-sized pieces. Develop one or two first steps for your goal and include any steps that you have already identified to remove any barriers that will prevent you from achieving your goal.

The first thing I will need to do to achieve my goal is:

1 _____

Other first steps are:

2 _____

3 _____

4 _____

5 _____

EXERCISE 8
EVALUATING OTHER COURSES OF ACTION

For each of the first steps identified in Exercise 7, use the pros and cons method (see page 106) to identify the way forward for those that have generated several possible choices:

Option 1	Pros	Cons	Conclusion
Option 2	Pros	Cons	Conclusion
Option 3	Pros	Cons	Conclusion

My preferred way forward is to:

EXERCISE 9
PLANNING THE PROJECT

Develop a project plan, using your diary to assist you to plan how you will allocate your time.

To consolidate your time, schedule sensible blocks into your plan according to the nature of the task.

If feasible, try scheduling certain tasks on particular days of the week and set aside parts of other days for working on major tasks. Alternatively, schedule different activities into the day according to your own best working pattern.

Work on the most important part of your project when your energy levels are at their highest, namely your 'prime time'. Identify how long you can concentrate on one thing at any one time – this varies from individual to individual.

Use your diary to:

plan each year first

> **plan each month next**

plan each week

> **plan each day at the outset**

EXERCISE 10
REVIEWING GOALS AND FIRST STEPS

Build regular review periods into your project plan for your goals and first steps. It is also useful to use the review process (see page 103) when something unexpected happens that might interfere with the smooth running of the project or the achievement of your goals.

Remember to focus on successes as well as problems. Things sometimes occur that can assist with your goal or project and these are as important to review as the barriers.

Ask yourself these questions:

'What is going well in relation to my goal?'

'What is not going so well in relation to my goal?'

'What has happened that might hinder the achievement of my goal?'

'Is there anything else I need to do to keep my project on track?'

'What has happened that might help with the achievement of my goal?'

'What adjustments do I need to make to my plan in the light of the answers to the above questions?'

'Do I need to seek help and if so, who might assist me?'

'When do I need to review my goals again?'

EXERCISE 11
INFLUENCING KEY STAKEHOLDERS

Throughout your project you will need to influence your key stakeholders and others who might become involved. Use the following method to make you more successful in influencing those people.

Work through the influencing checklist in Section 2 (see page 53) to help you plan your conversation. Remind yourself of the five assertive skills (see page 55), and then find a friend with whom to practise your situation. Ask for their feedback and use the lists below to check that your behaviour is assertive, rather than aggressive, passive or manipulative.

When I'm being **assertive:**

- I say what I want clearly and concisely.
- I make decisions for myself.
- I don't get put down.
- I stand up for my rights without violating others.
- I treat myself and others with complete respect and equality.
- I realize I am responsible for my own actions and feelings.
- I apologize when I have genuine regret.
- I am tough and 'stick to my guns' appropriately.
- I express my opinions, needs and wants and listen carefully to other people's opinions.
- I am calm, relaxed and confident.
- I feel energetic, powerful, confident and satisfied.
- I expect 'win/win' in disagreements.

When I'm being **passive:**

- I don't say what I want.
- I go along with other people's decisions.
- I allow others to bully, coerce and ridicule me.
- I deny my rights and allow them to be violated.
- I don't accept responsibility for what is happening to me.
- I find it hard to clearly express opinions, needs or wants.
- I often put myself down.
- I have difficulty making eye contact and I can be hesitant and nervous.
- I feel frustrated, powerless, unhappy, hurt and anxious.
- I expect 'lose/win' in disagreements.

When I'm being **aggressive:**

- I say what I want, often demandingly and at length.
- I make decisions for others.
- I bully, cajole and coerce.
- I blame, attack and violate other people's rights.
- I treat others with less respect.
- I take responsibility for others.
- I say 'I'm sorry but ...' and attack.
- I express opinion as fact and don't listen to others.
- I can be dominating, sharp and brusque.
- I feel energetic, angry, frustrated and powerful.
- I look for 'win/lose' in disagreements.

When I'm being **manipulative:**

- I am indirect and expect people to know what I want.
- I drop hints.
- I wheedle, flirt, falsely flatter and sulk.
- I am sarcastic.
- I manipulate people by playing on their feelings – often guilt.
- I behave passively with aggressive intention.
- I feel frustrated, angry and powerless.
- I often find 'lose/lose' in disagreements.

EXERCISE 12
USING SKILLS

Regularly return to Section 2 to review the skills Resource Pack that will help you to be successful in implementing your projects. Be honest with yourself and ask others for feedback on your strengths and weaknesses.

Ask yourself these questions:

'Whom might I ask to help me with this?'

'Do I need to develop any further skills? If so, what skills do I need to develop?'

'Are there any skills I could be using more?'

'How might I develop these skills?'

EXERCISE 13
GETTING REGULAR EXERCISE

In Section 2, we looked at how important it is to manage your stress and maintain a healthy lifestyle (see page 84). When working on projects, however, it can be difficult to remember to make time for some of the things that we know keep us healthy. A common omission is exercise. We become absorbed in a project and then forget to take regular exercise.

Exercise can make an enormous difference to your energy levels and motivation. Even a small amount of exercise during a break can mean the difference between re-applying yourself to your work afterwards and feeling demotivated or discouraged, and wanting to give up.

CHANGING YOUR LIFESTYLE

The problem with exercise is that we often feel that we need to go out of our way to build it into our lives – for example, by paying a visit to the gym or arranging a game of tennis with a friend. However, the most effective way of undertaking exercise is to build increased activity into your daily routine. It is important to select an exercise routine that suits your lifestyle; otherwise you will find it difficult to motivate yourself to do exercise. Find a friend to exercise with if you find it hard to motivate yourself.

BUILDING EXERCISE INTO YOUR ROUTINE

Here are a few things that you can do to build exercise into your daily routine with minimum effort. Make sure that you only exercise to a level with which you feel comfortable. Build exercise into your project plan – 20 minutes three times a week is a good starting point. Select one or more of the following options.

- Increase your walking pace, and go for a brisk 10–20 minute walk every other day.
- Always walk if you have to travel less than a kilometre (half a mile).
- Climb 50 steps each day; use stairs instead of escalators or lifts.
- Attend an exercise class in your lunch break.
- Buy a popular exercise video and practise it regularly at the beginning or end of the day.
- When you take a break from your project, build in some exercise rather than any other activity.
- Make exercise a habit.

EXERCISE 14
PRACTISING RELAXATION FOR STRESS RELIEF

Relaxation is a way of managing stress in the short term; the following exercise can be practised when sitting in a chair. It only takes 5 minutes to complete and can help you to relax at any time of the day when you find your stress levels reaching an unacceptable peak. It is particularly useful in the middle of the day as a 'pick-me-up', or when you are taking a break from your project.

Step 1

Find a quiet place where you can sit comfortably. Make sure you are free from interruptions. Make sure your arms and legs are not crossed, and get comfortable.

Step 2

When you are comfortable, close your eyes and consciously relax all your muscles, starting at the top of your head, down through your forehead, mouth, jaw, neck, shoulders, and so on. Become conscious of each muscle group as you relax them. Relax right down to your toes. Try to get into each group of muscles and imagine that you are going deeper... and deeper... into a deep relaxation. Take plenty of time.

Step 3

While you are relaxing, start breathing in deeply through your nose and out through your mouth. Listen to your breathing and notice that, as you relax, your breathing becomes deeper... and deeper. Enjoy the luxury of relaxing while you listen to your breathing. Notice the length of the pauses as you breathe out and before you breathe in.

Step 4

Continue to breathe deeply, maintaining all your muscle groups in a state of relaxation. As you do, begin to count backwards from 10 to 1 in the pauses. So, breathe out – 10; breathe in – 9; breathe out – 8; and so on. Repeat the exercise, counting from 1 to 10.

Step 5

Remain seated for a few minutes in your chair, keeping all your muscles relaxed and breath calmly. When you are ready, open your eyes and gently stand up.

EXERCISE 15
GIVING YOURSELF TREATS

Being able to treat yourself is a necessary part of keeping focused on your goals, and it ensures that you reward yourself during and after the completion of your project. Treats are a way of celebrating success. Setting yourself high standards is important in achieving your projects, but rewarding yourself for meeting your standards is equally important.

Treats are the rewards or gifts that we give ourselves for achieving success, or for cushioning the negative effects of failure. It is important to treat yourself both when things are going well and when things are tough.

Treats don't have to be big, or expensive; they can be little things, like watching your favourite movie, reading a chapter of a book you are enjoying, or taking your dog for a long walk.

1 Make a list of all the treats you enjoy.
2 Go to your project plan and block out periods of time for treating yourself.
3 Make this a habit.

If you find it hard to think of treats, as some of us do, ask your friends and colleagues how they treat themselves and try out some of their ideas.

EXERCISE 16
EVALUATING SUCCESS

When your project is almost complete, it is important to evaluate your achievements against the success criteria that you set at the beginning of the project. To do this, you need to return to your goal and look back at your achievements. This will enable you to sign off some of the aspects of your project and set in place other actions to ensure that any outstanding tasks are completed.

Step 1
Revisit your goal.

Step 2
Choose appropriate headings under which to describe your success. These can include the success criteria that you identified at the beginning of the goal-setting process. Choose the headings that are meaningful to you.

Step 3
List your achievements under each heading. Remember that, because you are behaving as if you have already achieved success, these notes will be written in the present or the immediate past tense.

- It is important to list as achievements those factors that may not yet be fully completed, as well as those you have successfully completed.
- Only include things you have been able to bring about directly, or at least influence considerably.
- Make your statements positive and specific and add in as much 'evidence' information as you can, to support your achievements.

Step 4

Identify the key events that led up to your success. These may include:

- Broad headings such as 'Qualifications', e.g. 'I was accepted on a Business Degree Course at college'.
- Each individual achievement, e.g. 'I have successfully employed a carpenter to build the new wardrobes in the dressing room'.
- Sensory achievements, e.g. how you feel or what you see.

Add in specific dates, who else was involved and 'evidence' information wherever possible.

Step 5

If necessary, set some more goals, with specific time-scales, to clear up any outstanding actions that have yet to be completed.

EXERCISE 17
CELEBRATING SUCCESS

Allow yourself the luxury of celebration when your project is complete. Do this as soon as possible after you have achieved your goals. In choosing a celebration, put yourself first, think big and luxuriate in your success. You deserve it!

If you really want something to happen, 'Just do it!'

A FINAL WORD

This book has introduced you to skills techniques and methods that, if applied to your projects and changes, will ensure that you achieve success. Putting the steps and skills described in the book into action involves hard work and dedication. It is important to choose the techniques that best suit your personality and methods of doing things, and it is important to remember that there is no right or wrong way of achieving your goals.

INDEX

accommodation, conflict response
60, 62
achievements, reviewing 139–40
action
  barrier removal 110
  choosing 106–8, 128
  handling stress 86
affirmation 40–1, 45
aggressive behaviour 48, 132
anger management 68–9
approaches
  conflict resolution 60–4
  goal-setting 98–9
assertiveness 46–57
  behaviour pattern 28–31, 131
  'change-back' avoidance 114–15
  development 51
  handling stress 84–5
  skills 55–6
authority, delegation 79
avoidance
  'change-back' 114–15
  conflict response 61, 63

barriers
  achievement 99, 101
  change 14–17
  delegation 81
  success 108–11, 124–5
behaviour
  aggressive 48, 132
  assertive 28–31, 46–57, 84–5, 114–15, 131
  changing 49
  handling stress 84
  manipulative 49, 55, 132
  passive 48, 132
  patterns 28–31, 131–2
  stress symptoms 83
breakdown, projects 99
breathing exercises 136–7

building self-esteem 88–91, 90
career change case study 7
  assertiveness 50
  domain maps 95
  force-field analysis 109–10
  priority setting 97
  success criteria 113
case studies 7, 9, 52
  see also career change; retirement plan; room change
  assertiveness 50, 54, 56–7
  change-back messages 114
  conflict 58–9
  domain maps 95
  fear management 44
  force-field analysis 109–10
  future mapping 100–1
  motivational factors 36
  moving house 52
  priority setting 97
  reviewing goals 104
  stakeholders 52
  stress handling 87
  success barriers 109–10
  success criteria 113
causes, stress 83
celebrating success 117, 141
challenges 40, 42, 121–2
change
  equation 8, 120
  motivators 9
  priorities 96–7
  risks 42
'change-back' messages 114–15
choices, actions 106–7, 128
co-operation 60–1
co-ordination, delegation 78
collaboration 61, 63
comfort zone 42–3
communication 74
comparisons, people 16, 39
competition, conflict response 60, 62

compromise 55–56, 61, 64
concentration 75
confidence building 39–41
conflict handling 58–65
  anger management 68–9
  approaches 60–4
  confrontation 66–7
confrontation
  conflict response 60–1
  fears 43, 45
  key skill 66–7
control
  stress handling 86–7
  success barriers 111
  time use 74
cost, change 8, 115
courses of action 106–8, 128
criteria
  identifying priorities 96
  success 112–13, 123, 139–40

daily planning 73
deadlines, delegated tasks 79
decision-making
  delegation 78
  priorities 96
delegation 74, 78–81
diaries 72–3
dissatisfaction 8, 94–5, 120
domain maps 94–5, 102, 120

effective working 77
elimination, unneeded tasks 74
emotions, handling stress 84
evaluation
  courses of action 106–7, 128
  success 139–40
exercise, physical 134–5
exercises 119–41
  change equation 120
  conflict assessment 64–5
  courses of action 128
  domain maps 120

evaluating success 139–40
first steps 127
force-field analysis 124
goal visualization 112
goal-setting 21, 122–3
influencing stakeholders 131
personal journal 20
planning 129
priorities 121–2
reflection 18–19
relaxation 136–7
reviewing goals 130
skills review 133
stakeholder analysis 125–6
stress management 136–7
success criteria 123
treats 138
willpower 38, 121
expression, anger 69
external self-esteem 88–91

factors
achievement 140
causes of stress 83
motivation 36
failure
coping 25
delegation 81
fear 16, 24–6
learning 20, 116–17
faster working 76
fear 42–4
failure 16, 24–6
management 45
feelings
see also fear
action evaluation 107
confrontation 66–7
failure 116
handling stress 84
fielding the response 55
first steps 102–5
change equation 8
identification, exercise 127
review, exercise 130
flexibility
goals 99

schedules 71
fogging technique 55
force-field analysis 108–9, 124
frustration management 68–9
future mapping 100

goals
importance 15, 21
reviewing 101, 103–4, 130
setting 98–101, 122–3
visualization 99, 100, 112
guidelines
delegation 81
goal-setting 100–1

identification
anger 68
first steps 102, 127
priorities 96–7, 121–2
skills 27–31
stakeholders 52, 125–6
success barriers 108–9
influence 28–30, 52–3, 131–2
initiative 46–51
inner voice 39–45
insulation, time use 74–5
internal self-esteem 88–9
inventory, skills 27–8
involving people 16, 100, 114, 125–6

journal 20

key skills see skills
knowledge
anger 69
project/change 71
stress 84

learning
cycle 103
from failure 20, 116–17
lifestyle 85, 134–5

management
anger and frustration 68–9
fear 45
stress 136–7

time 16, 32, 70–7
manipulative behaviour 49, 55, 132
margin for error 71
meetings 53, 76
mental pictures 99, 100, 112
monthly planning 72
motivation 9, 22, 36
moving house case study 52

negative inner voice 39–45

organization, delegation 78

passive behaviour 48, 132
past projects 19
perfectionists 24
personal portfolio 18
behaviour patterns 31
courses of action 106–7
failures 26, 116
personal journal 20
procrastination 23
skills 27
strengths and weaknesses 33
success criteria 112
physical exercise 134–5
planning 70–3, 101
delegation 78
exercise 129
first steps 102
positive messages 40–1
positive qualities 27–8, 41
priorities
identifying 96–7, 121–2
importance 15, 16
tasks 32
time 70–7
procrastination 23, 74

reactions, failure 25–6
reasons
change 9
stress 83
recognising anger 68
reflection, past projects 18–19
relaxation 136–7

epetition, assertive skill 55
resolution, conflict 60–4
resources, planning 71
responses, conflict 60–1
responsibility 14, 23, 79
retirement plan case study 7
   change-back messages
     114
   fears 44
   future mapping 100–1
   reviewing goals 104
   stress management 87
   success criteria 113
review
   delegated tasks 78, 79
   failures 116–17
   first steps 105
   goals 101, 103–4, 130
   skills 133
rewards 41, 117, 138
risk 42–5
room change case study 9
   assertiveness 54, 56–7
   conflict 58–9
   success criteria 113

saving time 76–7
scheduling 71, 129
self-discipline 17, 38
self-disclosure 56
self-enhancing thoughts 41
self-esteem 16
   behaviour factor 46–9
   maintaining 88–91
   negative messages 39
self-knowledge 13–33
setting goals 15, 21, 98–101,
   122–3
skills 17, 35–91
   anger management 68–9
   assertiveness 46–57, 55–6
   conflict management 58–65
   confrontation 66–7
   delegation 78–81
   fear management 39–45
   identification 27–33
   motivation 36–8
   organizational 15
   personal portfolio 27

self-esteem 88–91
stress management 82–7
time prioritizing 70–7
using 133
will-power 36–8
SMART objectives 98
specificity
   assertive skill 55
   goals 99
stakeholders
   identifying 52, 125–6
   influencing 53, 131–2
   involvement 16, 114
standards
   delegated tasks 79
   self-esteem 16, 39, 90
strategies
   barrier removal 111
   'change-back' avoidance
     114–15
   coping with failure 25
   fear management 45
strengths, assessment 27–33,
   41
stress 82–87, 136–137
stressors 83
success
   barriers 108–11,
     124–5
   celebrating 117, 141
   criteria 112–13, 123
   evaluation 139–40
   reflection 20
   stages 93–117
support networks 85
symptoms
   anger 68
   stress 82–3

thinking big 99–100
thinking time 77
time
   management 16, 32, 70–7
   saving 76–7
treats 117, 138

vision, change equation 8, 120
visualization 99, 100, 112

weaknesses, assessment 18,
   27–33
weekly planning 73
willpower 17, 22, 36–8, 121
work
   delegation 79
   simplifying 74

year planning 72

Acknowledgements

Executive Editor: Trevor Davies
Editor: Emma Pattison
Executive Art Editor: Rozelle Bentheim
Design: Martin Topping at 'ome
Illustrator: David Beswick at 'ome
Production Controller: Nigel Reed

The author

Ann Jackman is an independent
management development consultant
with a wide range of clients in both
the public and private sectors. She
runs her own company, AFJ
Associates in the UK, as well as
working in other countries. She
specializes in mentoring top and
senior managers; team development;
management development
programmes for directors and senior
managers, including 360-degree
feedback and action learning; and life
and career planning.